THE BOOK OF
REVELATION

CHARLES M. LAYMON

THE BOOK OF REVELATION

its message

and

meaning

ABINGDON PRESS — NEW YORK • NASHVILLE

THE BOOK OF REVELATION

Copyright © 1960 by Abingdon Press

Library of Congress Catalog Card Number: 60-10911

SET UP, PRINTED, AND BOUND BY THE
PARTHENON PRESS, AT NASHVILLE,
TENNESSEE, UNITED STATES OF AMERICA

This book is dedicated
to my daughter and two sons

SARAH MILDRED — DOUGLAS BURCH — JOHN BROOKS

PREFACE

The book of Revelation holds a unique position among Christians today. It is at one and the same time the most revered, the most misunderstood, and the most neglected of New Testament writings. From the first it has aroused discussion. Not all sections of the church accepted it as scripture in the beginning, but it ultimately found a place in the canon because of its inherent worth. Its inspired insights and spiritual fervor could not be denied— nor can they in our time among those who will take measures to understand it.

Due to its individualistic character, the Revelation to John may easily be misread in its moving passages by the beginner. Confused because of unfamiliarity with its symbolism and dramatic representations, he may turn from it, concluding that here is a book intended only for specialists. Not so. It was written for the entire body of church members and not for a particular group, and it may still be read with understanding by the laity.

When asked by Philip whether he understood the scriptural passage he was reading, the Ethiopian eunuch replied, "How can I, unless someone guides me?" The same question is frequently raised by those who undertake to read the Revelation for the first time. The present volume is written in an attempt to meet this need. It seeks to do this not only by interpreting the major individual passages of the Apocalypse, but also by relating them to one another so that the reader may grasp the message and meaning of the book as a whole.

7

METHODS OF INTERPRETATION

Through the centuries various approaches have been made to the interpretation of the book of Revelation. In modern times certain ones have become so standardized that definite names are assigned to them. First of all there is the *futurist* method. Persons of this school regard the book as portraying the events that immediately precede the end of the world. Here lies its purpose and significance. The entire writing, with the exception of the first five chapters, remains to be fulfilled.

Then there is the *preterist* approach that interprets its passages primarily in terms of the destruction of Jerusalem and the fall of the Roman Empire.

A third type of interpretation is the *continuous-historical* method. Up to a point it parallels the *preterist* approach; however, it moves beyond the fall of Rome and regards the Revelation as containing a summary of the entire history of the church and the world from the period of the writing of the book to the close of time. Events within the church and history are, accordingly, related to what are considered as corresponding passages in the book.

Finally there is the *symbolical* approach. This view suggests that the eternal principles of the prophecies should be deduced and then applied to the ongoing issues of life. These include such matters as the struggle of righteousness with evil, the fact and nature of judgment, and the final state of the faithful in a life of beatific blessedness. In ascertaining the eternal principle that the book contains, its various symbols and forms are analyzed and interpreted. To the extent that symbols and myth are related, this may be referred to as a demythologizing process.

My own approach in these pages is based upon an adaptation of the *preterist* and the *symbolical* methods. The passages in the Revelation are interpreted first of all in relation to their immediate background in the time of the emperor Domitian (A.D. 81-96), both literary and historical. Then their message, in principle, for all time is suggested.

A TIMELESS AND TIMELY MESSAGE

One of the characteristics of scripture is that because it is time-less, it is always timely. This is abundantly true of the book of Revelation. Written in a distant day and using a highly individual-istic vernacular, it, nevertheless, speaks to the present hour with a relevance that is undeniable. The message that it asserts comes home to us with particular pertinency.

When this writing insists that the universe is moral at heart and that God will use its forces in the punishment of evil men, nations, and spirits, it is uttering a word that modern man must heed anew in an age of nuclear power and unbelievable ventures in space. In its emphasis upon the authority of Christ—both in history and beyond history—it speaks directly to the Christian conscience as it faces competing claims of authority today. When it stresses the significance of suffering for righteousness' sake, it both inter-prets the experience of many in this century and challenges all in the present and future.

The supreme message of the book of Revelation is its assurance that Christ will emerge in history at long last as King of kings and Lord of lords. His victory will be the victory of all who place their trust in him. Thus there is purpose in living and hope in dying. The prospect of a transcendent revelation of Christ in power over evil in the future—whatever its form or nature—gives a new significance to all the tomorrows that time will bring.

In the writing of this book I am indebted to numerous persons who have labored magnificently in the field of apocalyptic litera-ture, and in the interpretation of the Revelation to John in par-ticular. The footnotes and bibliography bear witness to this debt. I would also mention the many students in my classes for this study through the years, whose response to its creative impact upon their own thought and faith was inspiring.

—CHARLES M. LAYMON

CONTENTS

PART I

THE BACKGROUND

CHAPTER ONE

The Biblical View of History:
Old Testament

The book of Revelation has captured the interest and imagination of its readers ever since it was written. Some are attracted to it because of its revelation of the future; others are intrigued by its symbolism and brilliant pageantry. Still others are greatly impressed by the sense of God and mystery that pervades the writing. But whatever the reason, a study of this New Testament document is an absorbing undertaking.

The individualistic character of the Revelation to John means that one cannot open it and begin to read its pages as one would with other books. Not only is new knowledge required, but also a special point of view in approaching it is necessary.

It is for this reason that we begin with a consideration of the biblical view of history, both in the Old and New Testaments. The Revelation is concerned with the end of time, with the events that lead to the close of history. Like the rest of the Bible, it has a particular understanding of history that modern historians as social scientists usually do not hold. Let us turn, therefore, to the subject of history as the Bible approaches and develops it. Only then will we be in a position to interpret the Revelation to John.

HISTORY IN OLD TESTAMENT TIMES

Almost from the beginning of human existence men have shown a concern for their life story. They carved their records on the rocks or scrawled them on the sides of the caves in which they lived. In time, legends and myths developed which bore the seeds of history and became the instruments of culture. These interpreted the past to the present so that it might better understand itself. From that distant day down to the present hour an interest in history has persisted.

This concern for human events did not escape biblical writers. They, too, recorded past happenings with verve and dramatic feeling. What the fathers had done was worth remembering. In Old Testament days it gave a kind of immortality to persons such as Samuel, David, and Solomon at a time when the Christian view of life after death had not yet come into being. In the first century of the Christian era, there were also those who felt impelled to put into writing the events in the ministry of Jesus. They went on to relate the story of the early days of the church in Jerusalem with the missionary expansion that followed.

It is customary to speak of certain of the Old Testament writings as the historical books. The list includes Joshua, Judges, Ruth, I and II Samuel, I and II Kings, I and II Chronicles, Ezra, Nehemiah, and Esther. They tell of the centuries following Moses when the Hebrews invaded Canaan, began to organize their scattered groups during the period of the judges, and eventually established their national life in the monarchy with Saul as their first king. The exploits of David, Solomon, Elijah, and Elisha are found here, as are also the backgrounds of the literary prophets. In addition there is an accounting of the tragic fall of Jerusalem with the deportation of the people to Babylonia as slaves. Their return to the homeland is also related, as well as the struggles that attended the rebuilding of their national life.

Not all Old Testament history, however, is found in the historical books. The writings of the Pentateuch (Genesis, Exodus, Leviticus, Numbers, and Deuteronomy) likewise reflect ancient life and times. Their traditional narratives reveal the customs and behavior of the early days, as well as the ideas and outlook of the writers at the time they were recorded. It is not always possible to separate the two, but this is not our concern here. Our interest is, rather, in pointing out the part that history played in the lives of men and women in biblical times. It was an important subject, almost the most important of all.

As traditional tales—those that had been handed down from the past—were related, the people of Israel found a new significance entering into their lives. They *belonged* to what had happened as well as to what was happening. A group consciousness was developing, and the worth of life as a member of this particular company became clearer while listening to accounts of the deeds of their forefathers. Living was important; and as inheritors of the past, they were important, too.

GOD AND HISTORY

Biblical history, sometimes called "salvation history," is uniquely written. In relating human happenings it includes divine elements with a naturalness that is disarming. At no time do the authors say, "We have been talking about man; now we shall speak of God." Man and God are seen as making history together. There is a constant interaction between them, and it is this that determines the outcome of events. Without God, in the biblical sense, there is and could be no history.

By contrast it is customary with us to omit God from the writing of history except to record the religious beliefs of peoples and races. We explain what occurred in the past, as well as what takes place today by referring to social, geographical, political, and economic factors. This is history that is written on the horizontal plane. Human motivation and decision alone are taken into account in interpreting historical developments. No place is made for a more than human causality in the social sciences, of which history is one. The idea that God has acted in, let us say, international relations is regarded as belonging to another discipline of thought such as philosophy, theology, or religion. History, it is felt, should limit itself to the human tale alone.

There are good reasons why the social scientist does this. His accepted tools for study consign him to the human sphere alone. But from the biblical point of view this sets limits to his task, and he can present only partial interpretations and explanations of human events.

In the Bible God is the chief character in history. It simply cannot be written abstracting him from the scene. Divine providence is not an addition that religious persons have introduced into the picture; it is structurally a part of everything that takes place. Sometimes it is interpreted so rigidly as to suggest a determinism from which man cannot escape.[1] Again it is represented as including human freedom where choices are made that affect the outcome of history.[2] But even here God is present in conditioning the results of the choices made.

BIBLICAL NARRATIVES

The early biblical narratives provide excellent illustrations of the approach that the Scriptures make to history. Although in some ways these may be said to be prehistorical in their typical use of myth and legend, nevertheless they charted the course that later historians followed. The Genesis stories show this clearly. In accounting for creation (1:1–2:24), the beginnings of sin (3:1-24), the source of the rainbow (9:8-17), and the origin of multiple languages (11:1-9), God is seen as the prime mover. No explanation would have been countenanced by the writers of these narratives that did not include him.

ABRAHAM AND THE COVENANT

The Abraham accounts are also quickened with this sense of something beyond that touches human life and makes history a divine as well as a human story.[3] For instance, it is in the establishing of the covenant between this patriarch and Jehovah that the origin of the national life of the Hebrews is explained. This was not interpreted by the early writers as a sociological and political pact that was made between the persons who were to live together in the new society. Instead, it was an agreement between

---

[1] Isa. 45:4-6.

[2] Cf. Matt. 23:37-39.

[3] It is recognized by most Old Testament scholars that the stories of the patriarchs represent early tribal and group experiences. Some would also hold that at the same time they tell of the exploits of individuals. This does not affect the points that are being made here in regard to the way biblical writers recorded the past.

God and his servant, and through this servant with the Hebrew people.

Because of God, Abraham left Haran in the first place and made the long journey to Palestine. This is how Genesis relates it:

Now the Lord said to Abram, "Go from your country and your kindred and your father's house to the land that I will show you. And I will make of you a great nation, and I will bless you, and make your name great, so that you will be a blessing. I will bless those who bless you, and him who curses you I will curse; and by you all the families of the earth will bless themselves."

—*Gen. 12:1-3*

When Abraham and his family reached the new country the promise was again reiterated in the form of a covenant:

When Abram was ninety-nine years old the Lord appeared to Abram, and said to him, "I am God Almighty; walk before me, and be blameless. And I will make my covenant between me and you, and will multiply you exceedingly." Then Abram fell on his face; and God said to him, "Behold, my covenant is with you, and you shall be the father of a multitude of nations. No longer shall your name be Abram, but your name shall be Abraham; for I have made you the father of a multitude of nations. I will make you exceedingly fruitful; and I will make nations of you, and kings shall come forth from you. And I will establish my covenant between me and you and your descendants after you throughout their generations for an everlasting covenant, to be God to you and to your descendants after you. And I will give to you, and to your descendants after you, the land of your sojournings, all the land of Canaan, for an everlasting possession; and I will be their God."

—*Gen. 17:1-8*

The biblical author wants us to see that the true beginnings of the Hebrew nation were to be found in the religious experience of the ancient patriarch. Later writings pick up the same theme; the Covenant plays an important part in the developing life of the people of God. Jesus himself was later to relate the Lord's Supper to it. In establishing the sacred meal he said, "This is my blood *of the covenant*,[4] which is poured out for many" (Mark 14:24).

JOSEPH AND DIVINE PROVIDENCE

The Joseph narratives also illustrate the biblical understanding of history. They are unparalleled examples of the conviction that divine providence rules and overrules the decisions of men, particularly in the face of misfortune and untoward circumstances. From the moment this favorite son of Jacob was sold into slavery, his life was beset by tragic difficulties. Betrayed by his brothers, maligned by an evil woman, jailed though innocent, he nevertheless rose to a position of personal eminence and became the savior of his own people—and of the Egyptians as well—in a time of calamity.

No more dramatic incident in the Old Testament can be found than the scene in which Joseph revealed himself to his brothers at the court of Pharaoh. Behind him were the years of suffering and success. Before him stood the brothers who had sold him into slavery because of jealousy. The tables were turned; at long last their fate lay in his hands. Now to right the wrong! Quite so. But how did Joseph do it? This is what he said:

"Come near to me, I pray you." And they came near. And he said, "I am your brother, Joseph, whom you sold into Egypt. And now do not be distressed, or angry with yourselves, because you sold me here; for God sent me before you to preserve life. For the famine has been in the land these two years; and there are yet five years in which there will be neither plowing nor harvest. And God sent me before you to preserve for you a remnant on earth, and to keep alive for you many survivors. So it was not you who sent me here, but God; and he has made me a father to Pharaoh, and lord of all his house and ruler over all the land of Egypt."

—*Gen.* 45:4-8

These words contain the biblical philosophy of history. God in his eternal purpose is here seen to be at work in the tangled and somewhat contradictory skein of human events. It is as Joseph says, "So it was not you who sent me here, but God; and he has made me a father to Pharaoh."

[4] Italics mine.

BIBLICAL HISTORICAL WRITINGS

Reference was made earlier in this chapter to the historical books of the Old Testament. They also tell the story of past events in terms that include God as well as man. The book of Judges, for example, applies what amounts to an almost moralistic formula in recording the life of the Hebrews in Canaan. These robust stories of Deborah, Gideon, and Samson in Israel's iron age are given a specific ethical setting. It is simple and direct: when the people and their leaders pleased Jehovah, they prospered and were victorious over their enemies; when they sinned he delivered them into the hands of their oppressors (Judg. 3:7-11; 4:1-3).

A further illustration of the nature of the historical writings in the Bible can be seen in the several books of Samuel, Kings, and Chronicles. Their object is not to present scientific history as we know it, but to sermonize in terms of past events. This is undergirded by the fact that in the Hebrew scriptures, Samuel, Joshua, Judges, and Kings are included in a section called "the former prophets." Although they contain historical materials of great value, the compiler's interest is largely theological. This interest grows out of the basic conviction that God is a part of history. He belongs here.

To illustrate: The historian points out that it was God who raised up Samuel to be a political and religious leader (I Sam. 3:1 ff.); at Jehovah's instruction Samuel chose Saul as king in spite of the fact that the Lord was not wholly in favor of it (I Sam. 10:20 ff.); in the end Jehovah rejected Saul because he disobeyed him (I Sam. 13:13-14). Surely this is an unusual manner of writing history.

One has only to speculate what it would be like if textbooks in American history were written in this fashion today to realize the special character of the biblical historian's method of recording past events. What new perspectives we might gain on Valley Forge, Gettysburg, and the Battle of the Bulge! Interpretation that reaches beyond the human scene to account for what takes place is basic to this procedure. Similar illustrations could be given from the recording of the exploits of David and the reign of Solomon as found in the historical writings of the Bible.

I and II Chronicles offer another excellent example of the way in which biblical history was written. The compiler who brought this material together, probably between 300 and 250 B.C., is best referred to as the Chronicler. He retold much of the story already found in Samuel and Kings, but he selected only those portions that would be of greatest interest to his contemporaries and of most value in expressing his own theological bent. He neglected the Northern Kingdom because its history was already known, and it had long since been destroyed. But Jerusalem and Judah were still a force in the life of the people. Some of the Chronicler's particular concerns, *which he saw history as validating*, were the truth of monotheism (I Chron. 29:10 ff.), the sin of idolatry (II Chron. 14:3 ff.), the omniscience of Jehovah (II Chron. 16:9), and his providential care of his chosen people as he speaks to them through Spirit-filled agents (I Chron. 17:1 ff.).

THE WRITINGS OF THE PROPHETS

The biblical attitude toward history is supremely illustrated in the writing of the prophets. They picture Jehovah as one who has been at work in the past, who is active in the present, and who will continue to labor in the future. Thus in Amos God is represented as inquiring, "Did I not bring up Israel from the land of Egypt, and the Philistines from Caphtor, and the Syrians from Kir?" (Amos 9:7.) The enslavement of the Hebrews in Babylon is viewed by Isaiah in moral rather than in political or military terms. It was a punishment for sin. At its close Deutero-Isaiah, speaking for Jehovah, can say,

> Comfort, comfort my peo-
> ple,
> says your God.
> Speak tenderly to Jerusalem,
> and cry to her

> that her warfare is ended,
> that her iniquity is pardoned,
> that she has received from the
> Lord's hand
> double for all her sins.
>
> —*Isa. 40:1-2*

Of particular interest in the prophetic view of history is the conviction that Jehovah can and does use nations other than the Hebrews to fulfill his purposes. He uses them even when they do not believe in him as their God and even though they do not know that they are his chosen instruments for executing his divine will. This was true in the case of Cyrus the Persian. Here the prophet's word to him from God was:

> For the sake of my servant Jacob,
> and Israel my chosen,
> I call you by your name,
> I surname you, though you do
> not know me.
> I am the Lord, and there is no
> other,
> besides me there is no God;
> I gird you, though you do not
> know me.
>
> —*Isa. 45:4-5*

The point in this situation is that Cyrus the Persian conqueror would soon overcome the king of Babylon. Then, as the new monarch, he would allow the Hebrews to return to their homeland. Both he and the Babylonians would explain this in military and governmental terms. But to the prophet it was a religious event involving more than human causes. Jehovah God was present and active in history. Paul Tillich has described this prophetic outlook in these words:

Here it is obvious that God reveals himself not only *in* history but also *through* history as a whole. The gods of space are overcome; history has a beginning, a center, and an end.[5]

THE PROPHETS DEPICT JEHOVAH'S KINGDOM

We have seen in the prophetic interpretation of history a deep belief in the activity of God in the past and present. What is of even greater significance is the prophet's expectation that Jehovah would reveal his will and power in the future. History was yet in the making and God would bring it to a glorious fruition or fulfillment.

It is of the end, or goal, of history that we are now thinking. There developed, under divine inspiration in Hebrew thought, a belief in the coming of Jehovah's kingdom. This was an expectation of an ideal society that would be raised up on earth. As such, it was eagerly anticipated by certain of the prophets and, in a popular way, by the people of the nation. From time to time the dream took different forms, but essentially it was to be an expression of the character of God as this was related to the affairs of men and nations.

One of these forms was the conception of the Day of the Lord (Amos 5:18). It was believed that a time would come when Jehovah would establish a divine rule in which his purpose in history would be realized. Evil men and nations were to be judged (Amos 5:18-20). But the faithful would be blessed (Isa. 51:3; 55:13; 60:13). A significant Old Testament passage that depicts this glorious day, the day when God would express himself in human society, represents the Eternal as saying:

> For behold, I create new heavens
>   and a new earth;
> and the former things shall not be
>   remembered
>   or come into mind.

[5] Paul Tillich, *The Protestant Era* (Chicago: University of Chicago Press, 1948), p. 22.

But be glad and rejoice for ever
    in that which I create;
for behold, I create Jerusalem a re-
        joicing,
    and her people a joy.

—*Isa. 65:17-18*

The importance of the Day of the Lord expectation as a back-ground for certain emphases in the book of Revelation will be evident when these are considered later. It is sufficient for the present to note their significance in connection with the prophetic view of history.

A historical outlook related to this day of the Lord expectation was the belief in a messianic age, involving such features as the glorification of the national life with the rule of the Messiah. Isaiah expressed it in this fashion:

Of the increase of his government
    and of peace
  there will be no end,
upon the throne of David, and over
    his kingdom,
  to establish it, and to uphold it
with justice and with righteousness
    from this time forth and for ever-
        more.
The zeal of the Lord of hosts will
    do this.

—*Isa. 9:7*

There was to be a universal reign of peace under this Davidic king (cf. also Isa. 11:7, 9).

During the hardships of the Exile (or captivity of the Hebrews in Babylon [586-538 B.C.]), this nationalistic conception of the goal of history fell into the background and gave way to the idea

25

of the redeemed and redeeming people of God. The latter were referred to as the Suffering Servant. Here salvation was wrought by the nation in travail (Isa. 52:13–53:12), or by the righteous remnant who remained faithful in the face of great odds (Isa. 10:20-23).

THE APOCALYPTIC HOPE

There was yet another form of messianic expectation involving a view of history that developed, partly under the influence of Persian religion, following the Exile. It was apocalyptic in character. Apocalyptic thought involves heavenly deliverance by a sudden intervention of God. It envisions cosmic disturbances, the overthrow of evil, and the blessing of the faithful. Visions and dramatic symbols are characteristic here.[6]

This view is particularly basic to the study of the Revelation to John. Because of the discouragement that the Hebrews felt while they lived under a succession of foreign conquerors, they began to think that their destiny depended upon some dramatic salvation from God *coming down from the heavens*. Whereas the messianic king and kingdom of Isaiah 7, 9, and 11 were expected to be raised up from among the Hebrew people, this particular apocalyptic deliverance would enter the plane of history from above.

It is in the book of Daniel that this type of messianic hope becomes prominent in the Old Testament scriptures. Antiochus Epiphanes, the Syrian ruler (175-163 B.C.), was oppressing the Hebrews unmercifully as he sought to force them into Greek cultural patterns. The author of Daniel urged the people to hold fast courageously and promised that deliverance would come:

> I saw in the night visions,
> and behold, with the clouds of
> heaven
> there came one like a *son of man*,[7]
> and he came to the Ancient of
> Days

[6] Cf. Chap. 3, pp. 45-49.
[7] Italics mine.

and was presented before him.
And to him was given dominion
and glory and kingdom,
that all peoples, nations, and
languages
should serve him;
his dominion is an everlasting
dominion,
which shall not pass away,
and his kingdom one
that shall not be destroyed.

—Dan. 7:13-14

The phrase "son of man," as found in this passage, is used in the Similitudes of Enoch, a noncanonical apocalyptic writing, in referring to an individual heavenly being, transcendent and exalted (I Enoch 46:3-4). Ezekiel employs it as a designation of the prophet himself (2:1 ff.). In Daniel, however, it is considered by most modern-day scholars to be a collective expression. As such it refers to God's saints, a renewed and glorified Israel coming to earth from the heavens. God would thus fulfill his purpose in history with a mighty deliverance and salvation. The expression also appears frequently in the New Testament.

We have seen in this chapter that history is a major theme in the Old Testament. It is written as the account of man's relation to his fellow men and to God and also as the account of God's movements within time. In traditional narratives, historical statements, prophetical documents, and apocalyptic writings, this story is told with bold ethical insight and a heightened sense of dramatic development.

We are now ready to turn to a consideration of the biblical view of history in the New Testament.

CHAPTER TWO

The Biblical View of History: New Testament

For an understanding of the New Testament view of history we must turn, first of all, to the developing Christian community, sometimes referred to as the early church. Its appearance was an epochal event that was regarded as the work of God himself. In this sense it is a divine society whose very existence judges other institutions. The purposes of creation and God's redemption in history are here revealed within the temporal world.

THE ORIGIN OF THE CHRISTIAN COMMUNITY

We have seen that in the Old Testament the accounts of the Hebrew people were written with the conviction that God was present in the affairs of men. Whatever part they played in historical events—and they did have a considerable role—in the final analysis it was God who controlled the outcome. History contained a serious expression of divine purpose. Sometimes this goal was conceived by the prophets as the messianic kingdom (Isa. 9:2-7; 11:1-10); again it was spoken of as the consummation that would attend the arrival of the Day of the Lord (Amos 5:18-20; Joel 2:28-32).

As has been indicated, we find, when we come to the New Testament, that the writers are convinced that the early church is the actual expression of God's purpose in history. It is the New Israel toward which past—that is, Old Testament—events had been moving. What had been a hope and an expectation had now actually come to pass. We can see this in Peter's sermon on Pentecost when the Holy Spirit came upon the assembled followers of Jesus

(Acts 2:14-36). In moving words he interpreted this ecstatic occurrence as a fulfillment of Joel's prophecy concerning the last days. The Spirit had indeed been bestowed upon all flesh; a new age had dawned in which ordinary men and women—not a special class such as the seers and prophets—would prophesy and in which both old and young would see visions.

This first fellowship of Spirit-filled believers was regarded as constituting an eschatological community. Eschatology is the science of final things. It usually includes such themes as judgment, the overthrow of evil, blessing for the righteous, and immortality. Used in this connection, it means that in the early church it was thought that the end of time or the end of days was near. The kingdom had not fully come, since greater revelations were in the offing. The return of Christ would introduce still fuller manifestations of the purpose and glory of God. But in the meantime what the Christian community was experiencing was not simply an Indian summer; it was genuinely real.

The main point to consider here is that this new community was regarded as God's own creation and, as such, was the Eternal's divine act in history. It *came upon* the first century, and even though it had historical antecedents and would yet have a historical development, human agencies did not originate it; God did!

CHRIST AND THE ORIGIN OF THE CHRISTIAN COMMUNITY

How did God call the Christian community into existence? The answer to this question is that he did so through Christ. Apart from him its beginning, as well as its continuance, was incomprehensible. But seen as stemming from his birth, life, death, and resurrection, and sustained by his spiritual presence, it was self-authenticating. He gave it being and character; he was its power and hope.

THE INCARNATION

The birth of Jesus, interpreted as the incarnation of God in human flesh, signaled the beginning of the New Day. It was within history that Christ came to live and die, only to rise again. His advent was foreseen by the prophets and recognized by the faithful. The sainted Simeon could take the Christ child in his arms and say that he was now ready to depart from this life, since he had witnessed God's salvation that had been prepared as a light to the Gentiles and a glory to Israel (Luke 2:29-32). Before this, the psalm of Zechariah, in which John the Baptizer is seen as a part of the age that is to be inaugurated, proclaimed the greatness of the redemption that was coming upon men with the birth of Jesus Christ:

> Blessed be the Lord God of Israel,
> for he has visited and redeemed his
>   people,
> and has raised up a horn of salva-
>   tion for us
> in the house of his servant David,
> as he spoke by the mouth of his
>   holy prophets from of old,
> that we should be saved from our
>   enemies,
> and from the hand of all who hate
>   us;
> to perform the mercy promised to
>   our fathers,
> and to remember his holy covenant,
> the oath which he swore to our
>   father Abraham, to grant us
> that we, being delivered from the
>   hand of our enemies,
> might serve him without fear,
> in holiness and righteousness be-
>   fore him all the days of our
>   life.
>   —*Luke 1:68-75*

God was moving to save.

THE LIFE OF JESUS CHRIST

It was not simply in the fact of Christ's advent, but also in the character of the life he lived, that God revealed his purpose through history. For this reason the New Testament is careful to indicate the kind of person Jesus Christ was. His story was not the typical Greek legend of the dying and rising of a god. Rather, it was the account of one whose quality of living made men conscious of God himself.

In the contact of the people with Jesus, they experienced the Eternal's holy love and power. He placed forgiveness, healing, renewal of mind, and restoration of self into their hands. The kerygma, or early Christian message, was saying just this when it told how God had anointed him "with the Holy Spirit and with power; [and] how he went about doing good and healing all that were oppressed by the devil" (Acts 10:38).

THE DEATH OF JESUS CHRIST

Not only does the life of Jesus Christ reveal God at work in history; his death was also a sign and seal of this fact. With great eloquence—and greater insight—the apostle Paul declared that in the Cross God's righteousness had been manifested. As slaves through the payment of a ransom are given their freedom, as guilty men who stand before the judge are pronounced innocent in a court of law, and as sinners are cleansed in traditional sacrifices, just so God has placed mankind in a position of redemption through the event on Calvary (Rom. 3:21-26). To be sure, men must react in faith to what happened there if they are to know this great salvation personally; but God himself has opened the way.

The revelation of God in history is a continuous theme in the Bible. This does not mean, however, that he is to be seen equally in all of the events that occur within time. Some are viewed as being more redemptive than others—and, therefore, more revealing. In the Old Testament the deliverance of the Hebrews from Egypt stands out supremely. By this act God made them his special people, and in this experience they accepted him as their very own

God. The New Testament, on the other hand, turns its light upon the Cross. Here is the break in the heavens through which God shows his face in love—finally, fully, and with great glory. It is in this sense that John Knox can refer to the Cross as "the *central moment* in a divinely creative and redemptive event." [1] This the church recognized, and this the church proclaims.

THE RESURRECTION OF JESUS CHRIST

Just as the death of Christ cannot be viewed apart from the life of devotion and vocation that preceded it, so the Cross must also be seen in relation to the Resurrection that followed. In a very real sense, apart from the Resurrection, the Cross would not have been the CROSS. Death became a prelude to life because on the first day of the week God raised Jesus Christ. In a cosmic act within history where death prevailed, God moved to overcome it. Death and time were transformed into life and eternity. Thus the physical order was shown to be subservient to the spiritual.

The author of Ephesians was deeply moved by the revelation of God in history through the Resurrection. He referred to it in terms of the newness of life that it brought to believers, and saw here "the immeasurable greatness of his [God's] power in us who believe, according to the working of his great might which he accomplished in Christ when he raised him from the dead and made him sit at his right hand in the heavenly places" (1:19-20).

In commenting upon this passage, Paul S. Minear has said, "Plainly this declares that God has overcome the relativity of all historical events in this one historical event of the death-resurrection of Christ." [2] Although he is always related to the events that occur within history, in a particular way in this case, from beyond time God acted within time and showed its true meaning. As men respond to this revelation they are made to be citizens of heaven.

It has been our purpose to show thus far in this chapter the

---

[1] John Knox, *The Death of Christ* (Nashville: Abingdon Press, 1958), p. 128. Italics mine.

[2] Paul S. Minear, *The Kingdom and the Power* (Philadelphia: The Westminster Press, 1950), p. 42.

relation of the birth, life, death, and resurrection of Jesus Christ to the origin of the Christian community. Not only do they, in themselves, point to God's redemption in history, but they also account for the beginning of the Church, a fellowship in Christ, no less. God called it into being through Jesus.

THE LIVING CHRIST, THE HOLY SPIRIT, AND HISTORY

We have noted that the New Testament regards the Christian community as the expression of God's purpose in history. *Behind* this community is Christ in his birth, ministry, death, and resurrection. Tremendous as this is, it is not all; there is a further fact. *Within* this community is Christ also. How did this come to be and how does it continue to be?

The first followers of Jesus were crushed to the earth by the crucifixion of their Lord. It seemed to mark the end of their fellowship with him and the termination of the hopes he had awakened in them that the kingdom of God was at hand. Dark hung the night in the heavens. But not for long. The Resurrection changed all this, as it convinced them that their Lord was alive. God had acted to overcome death and the evil that men do. The kingdom would yet come on earth, even as it is in heaven.

It is difficult to imagine—and yet we must attempt it—the ties that bound together these first witnesses to the Resurrection. Theirs was a very special kind of experience, unlike any known on earth. They were marked men—and women, too—since the marks of the living Christ were upon them. It shone in their faces, their gait, and their talk. The fact that only a limited number of persons had experienced the Presence set them apart from the rest. They were "in"; others were "out." This exclusiveness gave them a kind of group consciousness that constituted a Resurrection fellowship. This, in fact, was the beginning of the Christian community or the early church.

The accounts of the Resurrection indicate that the disciples' experience of the presence of Christ was intermittent. Luke summarizes the situation by saying that, "to them he presented himself alive after his passion by many proofs, appearing to them during forty days, and speaking of the kingdom of God" (Acts 1:3). The apostle Paul also presents a list of appearances in his correspondence with the Corinthian church. They were to Cephas, the twelve, a group of more than five hundred, James, and then again to all the apostles (I Cor. 15:5-7). Paul also included himself, but I did not name him here because this probably refers to his Damascus Road conversion, which occurred several years later. There are those who feel, however, that it was of the same kind as the earlier resurrection experiences.

In addition to the Corinthian listing of the resurrection appearances, we have the references in the Gospels. There seems to have been no continuity in this situation. Appearance and disappearance were evidently the rule. It would have been difficult to build a church on this basis.

At Pentecost all this was changed. The realization of the presence of the living Christ became a constant possession of the church through the indwelling of the Holy Spirit whom he sent to his waiting followers at Jerusalem (Acts 2:1-42). I do not mean that they were always aware of him as the present Lord; their sensitivity probably varied from time to time, even as does ours. But now in the Christian community there was a steady consciousness of the living Christ's abiding in their midst rather than a series of appearances and disappearances. All of this was possible because the Holy Spirit and the Spirit of Christ were one in the experience of New Testament Christians (cf. Acts 16:6-7; Rom. 8:9-10; II Cor. 3:17).

The consequences in history of the reality of the presence of Christ through the Holy Spirit are demonstrated again and again in the New Testament. Its writings not only abound in references to this fact; it is also in the very texture of the sentences, since it was a presupposition of the writers themselves. The remark that the Acts of the Apostles might quite properly have been named the Acts of the Holy Spirit, because of the predominate emphasis upon his guidance of the developing church, bears witness to this truth. For instance, its expansion through the missionary movement is credited to the Holy Spirit. Luke notes that it was while they were praying at Antioch, "worshiping the Lord and fasting," that the Holy Spirit said, "Set apart for me Barnabas and Saul for the work to which I have called them" (Acts 13:2).

What does this mean? It indicates that the living Christ through the working of the Holy Spirit is a dynamic factor in history. We have here an active Cause, beyond human causality, present in the affairs of men and nations. History that is written as the story of man alone is only partly true. Christ must be included henceforth; he is to be reckoned with in assessing human direction and destiny.

THE OUTCOME OF HISTORY

We have seen that the work God had undertaken in history through the Christian community, founded by Christ and continually quickened by his presence through the Holy Spirit, represented the Eternal's purpose in creation and redemption. This conclusion as drawn by the early church was rooted and grounded in experience. The new life was a fact that needed only to be interpreted; and this is what we find the writers of the New Testament undertaking to do.

When we say that the authors were *interpreting* their experiences in the Christian community, we are not suggesting a purely rationalistic process. First of all, the persons who wrote of these matters were themselves a part of the situation they were interpreting. They had to write because they had been captured by Christ. The apostle Paul, who penned, roughly speaking, about half the New Testament, said of himself, "I have been crucified with Christ; it is no longer I who live, but Christ who lives in me." In writing of the new life in Christ, such a person would himself be engrossingly and wonderfully involved. He would know personally the glory of which he wrote.

In the second place, the Holy Spirit was at work in the lives of the authors of the New Testament. In the preceding section we took note of his dynamic relation to the new community in Christ, of his quickening and life-giving power in the experience of those who looked by faith to Christ for their salvation. This same Spirit was illuminating the minds of the writers of the Gospels and epistles.

Thus they were inspired by the Spirit as they interpreted the things of the Spirit for those who had been caught up in the life of the Spirit.

This does not mean that the minds of those who wrote of the faith were inactive as they sought to make clear its meaning. A close reading of their writings will show that, at one and the same time, they were creatively alert to the situations they were facing and thoughtfully sensitive to the facts of the Gospel. The incisiveness with which they reported, illustrated, and set forth the events of which they were a part, so that timeless truths were not lost in the immediate issues, marks them as persons of true intellectual stature.

It is important that we realize the dynamic character of the situation within which the authors of the New Testament wrote as we approach their interpretation of the outcome of history. It is one thing to write of matters immediately at hand; it is another to look into the future and envision the ultimate end of the story. The popular mind would most likely interpret the latter as crystal gazing. This is incorrect as far as the New Testament is concerned. What we have here is more a realization or sensing of the truth that since one thing is so, another must follow in what lies ahead.

Because the early church considered the future on the basis of its present redemptive experience, history and the moral life were seen as interrelated. *This meant that the outcome of events must be in line with the character of God as revealed in Christ.* In arriving at this conclusion there was more than a process of reasoning at work. We may call it a spiritual or moral intuition, but by whatever name it is known, it is basic to all New Testament thought regarding the future. This is quite different from fortune-telling.

For some authors these ideas were accompanied by ecstasy and visions that were later put into words in true apocalyptic fashion. Symbolic phrases, traditional figures of speech, and original thought forms combined to describe what was to be. Others simply referred to the future in terms of the realization of Christian ideals without attempting any detailed pictorialization of coming events.

Both of these approaches are to be found in New Testament scriptures. No doubt there were those who took the form of the description of future events more literally than others. Yet, the fact that the writers did not seriously attempt to harmonize their accounts suggests that they did not regard the details too seriously. Certainly for us it is not the way the truth is expressed, but the truth itself, that is central.

THE EXPECTATION

In considering the New Testament's expectation concerning the outcome of history, we shall base our thinking upon references outside the book of Revelation, since the latter will be treated at length later in the book. Broadly speaking, this will not seriously alter the conclusions that are drawn, for at heart the Apocalypse is basically in harmony with the rest of the thinking of the New Testament upon this theme. There is a oneness of message throughout.

This oneness grows out of the fact that the writers of the early church customarily treated the same themes as they considered the outcome of history. These included the return of Christ, victory over all evil men and forces on earth and in the spirit world, the resurrection of the dead, the final judgment, and eternal blessing for the faithful. As we shall see in the next chapter, with the exception of the return of Christ there was an inherited pattern here; these were the subjects that were customarily found in Hebrew apocalyptic. Traditionally they had been considered appropriate to such discussions.

There were, however, marked differences between early Christian thinking and Hebraic thinking upon these matters. These were due to the fact that Christ was always in the center of Christian thought. He dominated the scene. It was Christ who would return; it was Christ who would overcome all evil; it was Christ who would call forth those who had fallen asleep; it was Christ who would judge both good and bad; it was Christ who would prepare the eternal dwelling; and it was in Christ's presence that the faithful would live forever. Whenever there are representations of the end of the world that seem to parallel earlier traditional portrayals, the introduction of Christ into the picture makes it a new and different expectation.

When the goal of history is viewed from the Christ-angle, it possesses a perspective that makes so great a difference that the outlook is unique. His character qualifies and determines the conception and course of events. In returning at the end of the age, Christ fortifies and reiterates the lordship he has already shown as a living presence in their lives (I Thess. 2:19; Gal. 2:20; Matt. 28:20). As the one in whom God's redemption is made real in the final kingdom, he accomplishes the full defeat of evil. This he had begun in his ministry, brought to a climactic expression in the Cross and Resurrection, and continued to perform as living Lord in the Christian community (Matt. 12:28; I Cor. 15:25). By calling forth the faithful who have already died, all shall have an opportunity to participate in the blessed life (I Thess. 4:15-16).

There is more. In the role of righteous judge, Christ will show his true character as Lord, both of the faithful and over the wicked: "We must all appear before the judgment seat of Christ, so that each one may receive good or evil, according to what he has done in the body" (II Cor. 5:10). This judgment will not be vindictive; it will come from the hands of One who has already given his life to save men and whose love is beyond doubting. But judgment is not an end in itself. For the wicked—and this is moral realism— it will lead to destruction (Matt. 25:31-46; John 5:29); however, the good will be blessed in the eternal presence of God (I Cor. 15:24-25, 58; I Thess. 4:17).

The New Testament conceives of the final consummation of history as the full realization of God's will. What he has revealed in time, what has actually been begun on earth in the birth, life, death, resurrection, and living lordship of Christ will be brought to its fulfillment through Christ and in Christ.

It is not clear just when or where this will take place. Certainly it is evident that within the New Testament it is believed that the end will be soon (I Thess. 4:15, 17; Phil. 4:5; Rom. 13:11-12). It may also be demonstrated that the writers sometimes thought of the triumphant kingdom in which the blessed lived with Christ as existing on earth (Matt. 25:21), while again they placed the scene in heaven (John 14:2-3). In addition there are references to new heavens and a new earth (II Pet. 3:13). The location is not the issue; it is triumph in Christ.

One last word. While all of these events occur in and through Christ, it is God the Father who is ultimate in the final outcome of history. The Son is Lord, but the Father himself is supreme. Paul's statement in this regard is so significant that it must be quoted:

Then comes the end, when he [Christ] delivers the kingdom to God the Father after destroying every rule and every authority and power. For he must reign until he has put all his enemies under his feet. The last enemy to be destroyed is death. "For God has put all things in subjection under his feet." But when it says, "All things are put in subjection under him," it is plain that he is excepted who put all things under him. When all things are subjected to him, then the Son himself will also be subjected to him who put all things under him, that God may be everything to every one.

—*I Cor. 15:24-28*

There is a glory and a finality to these words which gives a significance to history that is without parallel in the religions of the world.

CHAPTER THREE

The Nature and Interpretation of Apocalyptic Literature

Since an apocalyptic writing such as the book of Revelation is concerned with the fulfillment of God's purposes in time, *particularly at the end of time when these issue in a climactic conclusion,* the question of the meaning of history is involved. It was for this reason that we looked at both the Old Testament and the New Testament views of history in the two preceding chapters. They provided a background for our present study.

HISTORY AND THE APOCALYPSE

We saw in this brief review that history was regarded as the scene of a drama of redemption in which God himself was active. As the one who created man, he had vigorously moved to save him in his sin. Jehovah God not only had an ideal for individual man when he made him in his own image; he also had in mind an ideal of a perfect society in which man would live.

Human agency had a place in establishing this new age or kingdom. God would use men if they responded to his call, a summons that came particularly through chosen vessels such as the prophets. When mankind in its sin failed to respond to the summons, the heavenly Father sent his Son. Through the birth, life, death, resurrection, and living presence of Christ the early church as a community of believing persons was created—a community that expressed God's purpose for his people. The Church was the sign and seal of the New Day that was actually beginning to appear within history. It had not yet fully arrived. But it would surely come to its fulfillment through a final intervention of God. The Divine would act; Christ would return, judge, and overthrow evil men, nations, and spirits and establish the final kingdom in which the faithful would be blessed forever.

It is here that the Revelation to John as an apocalyptic writing comes into the picture. It presents a portrayal of the end of history. At the close of the previous chapter we indicated what some of the other New Testament writings had to say on this subject. For all their significance—and it is considerable—it is to the book of Revelation that we must turn for our fullest and greatest treatment of this theme. No other apocalyptic writing, either within or without the New Testament, can equal this tremendous presentation.

THE MEANING OF APOCALYPSE

As an apocalyptic writing, the Revelation to John must be interpreted in a particular fashion. It is important to realize this and face it from the very beginning. Not to do so would be fatal—as fatal as to attempt to read poetry as prose or legal documents as fiction. In either case the result would be hopelessly misleading.

Perhaps this is the reason many find the Apocalypse difficult. Some are so confused by what they read that they give it up as a useless undertaking. The right key placed in their hands would make a tremendous difference and save the book for them as a source of spiritual inspiration.

At the opposite pole are the uninformed persons who read it with a kind of swashbuckling determination, making pious guesses as to its meaning, and come to be fanatics. Most of today's Christians tend to find themselves in either one or the other of these categories.

This need not be the case. There is a way to read the Revelation to John so that it will speak to our own time and to us individually. First of all, it is necessary to know something about the apocalyptic outlook and the apocalyptic forms of expression. It is also important to become familiar with the background against which this exciting book was written. It is to the first of these needs that we shall turn in this chapter and to the second in the chapter that follows it.

When we say that the Revelation to John is an apocalyptic writing or an "apocalypse," what do we mean? The word apocalypse comes from a Greek term *apokalupsis* which indicates a revelation or unveiling of that which has heretofore been hidden and mysterious. In such a writing the veil is torn away, present facts are interpreted, and the future—usually the immediate future—is revealed. Some persons may claim that they do not wish to learn what is to happen, but there are more who are really interested in future events. We like to know where we are going, and the clarification of heavenly secrets seems filled with promise. This is one reason that the prospect of the apocalyptic appeals to us.

Reference has just been made to future events with the statement that this is the concern of an apocalypse. You might well inquire, therefore, what is the difference between prophecy and apocalyptic pronouncements? The answer is that while both are interested in the future, prophecy sees the New Day coming largely through regular historical channels, involving changes in the social and political scene. The apocalyptic, however, looks toward heavenly and miraculous agencies at work with a kind of cosmic and revolutionary intrusion into the human plane. This is more dramatic and startling than the prophetic; it is high voltage in the extreme.

There is yet another word that must be understood in this connection. It is eschatology. It comes from the Greek word *eschatos* meaning last [days], or the end [of what is spoken of]. In Christian usage it may refer to such matters as the end of the world (John 6:39-40), or to the last or latter days (Heb. 1:2). The Revelation to John is an eschatological writing in the sense that it deals with the last days involved in the outcome of history and the end of time. As a rule, the subjects found in an eschatological discussion include such matters as death, the judgment, the end of history, and immortality. All find a place in the Apocalypse.

WHAT HAPPENS TO HISTORY?

At this point it will be helpful to look at four views of history in order to highlight the uniqueness of the apocalyptic, which is itself a view of history. The first envisions history as a cycle of events repeating itself over and over. It is usually regarded as having been held by the Greeks. There is little or no progress to this outlook. Life continues to move round and round, and a discussion of the end of time does not seem to be in order here.

The evolutionary view of history should be mentioned next. It is an application of a biological principle to social fields and holds that through gradual development history moves along progressively toward ever higher expressions. To be sure, the process is sometimes more accelerated than at other periods. There are also setbacks and dead ends along the way. But the rule is ever onward toward the better day. This view was quite widely held during the early decades of this century.

A third view of history is that which is claimed by the communists. It rests on the thinking of Karl Marx and the philosophy of Hegel. Sometimes it is called economic determinism, since economic goals predominate and the outcome of events is considered as predetermined. Hegel viewed life as moving from one extreme (thesis) to another (antithesis) but finally resting upon a midway station (synthesis) between them. In communist thought the victory of their cause is believed to be certain, since it is regarded as grounded in this movement of events. Thus, it is felt, history will march inevitably to the victory of communism throughout the world. Revolution will bring this to pass as a part of the formula.

The fourth view of history and its outcome is the apocalyptic. It is unlike the three preceding views, as it holds that mankind will grow increasingly evil until it is necessary for God to intervene from beyond. He will abruptly and decisively interrupt the course of history by an act, or a series of acts, that will bring it to a close. Evil men and nations have become intolerable to the Almighty; the case for goodness seems destined to be lost—unless he steps in and stops the movement of events. Therefore, since his cause is at stake and the purposes of creation hang in the balance, he must act. The apocalyptist, accordingly, envisions this mighty drama of the end.

THE PHILOSOPHY AND PSYCHOLOGY OF APOCALYPTIC THOUGHT

There is both a philosophy and a psychology behind the apocalyptic view of history. First of all, its philosophy is based on the conviction that this is a moral universe in which goodness counts. It makes a difference not only in human relationships but also in human destiny. Men cannot play fast and loose with God's will; or, as we say, "the piper must be paid." Repentance and faith in Christ will avail here.[1] But where these do not exist, evil's bitter fruit must be eaten. A last chance is real; judgment is certain; the end of time will come; history will be concluded!

The psychology that is active in an apocalyptic view of history is equally rooted in moral conviction. When the evils of existence become unbearable, men look beyond themselves for deliverance, not only because they are desperate, but also because they will not give up their belief in the goodness of God.

We can see this philosophy and psychology illustrated in the book of Daniel. The situation behind the writing of this Old Testament book was one of great persecution and suffering on the part of the Jews. Antiochus Epiphanes, the Syrian king who ruled over them during the period 175-163 B.C., was attempting to force Hellenistic culture upon them. He went so far as to erect an altar to Zeus in the Temple. In keeping with this act he ordered that the circumcision of children, the offering of sacrifices to Jehovah, the observance of food laws, and the keeping of the Sabbath should cease. Even the copies of the Hebrew scriptures were to be confiscated and destroyed. Those who would not comply with these edicts were put to death.

What to do? Where to look? What to expect? The author of Daniel turned to the outlook of apocalyptic in this crisis. He insisted that the Jews should remain faithful, even as Daniel had done. Was he not delivered? Then there were the three friends in the fiery furnace; they, too, were saved, even though they were tried by fire. God would also act to redeem the Jews. Antiochus

---

[1] I am thinking of *Christian apocalyptic* in this particular remark. Hebrew apocalyptic would not give to Christ this position.

would be overthrown, and the Eternal would establish his kingdom through the descent from heaven of a purified and redeemed community. Here the faithful would be blessed.

Wherever you find apocalyptic writing, thinking such as this is behind it. Desperation and faith combine to impel men to the crucial conviction that God will move to save. Earthly help is regarded as of no avail in these situations. Man cannot act; he can only be faithful and trust. This, however, is not regarded as giving up; it is considered to be the most active kind of believing. It is faith under fire.

THE NATURE OF APOCALYPTIC WRITINGS

We have considered the philosophy and psychology that give rise to the apocalyptic outlook, as well as the relation of this outlook to prophecy, history, and eschatology. Now we shall attempt to answer the question, "What kind of writing grows out of apocalyptic thinking?"

UNIQUE REPRESENTATIONS

When one opens the pages of the Apocalypse to John and begins to read, it does not take long to discover that here is a different kind of writing. Unfamiliar representations abound. But it is not only the expressions that are strange; the scenes they portray involve unearthly activities in which figures beyond everyday experience predominate. Take such a passage as the following:

> And round the throne, on each side of the throne, are four living creatures, full of eyes in front and behind: the first living creature like a lion, the second living creature like an ox, the third living creature with the face of a man, and the fourth living creature like a flying eagle. And the four living creatures, each of them with six wings, are full of eyes all round and within, and day and night they never cease to sing,
> "Holy, holy, holy, is the Lord God
> Almighty,

who was and is and is to come!

—*Rev. 4:6b-8*

Still another reference will illustrate the unusual character of apocalyptic portrayal:

And this was how I saw the horses in my vision: the riders wore breastplates the color of fire and of sapphire and of sulphur, and the heads of the horses were like lions' heads, and fire and smoke and sulphur issued from their mouths.

—*Rev. 9:17*

But there is more. The use made of numbers is unique. For instance there are twenty-four elders (4:4), seven seals to be broken (5:1), 144,000 sealed (7:4), a third of the sea becomes blood (8:9), the holy city will be trampled on for forty-two months, while the two witnesses prophesy for 1,260 days (11:2-3), and the number of the beast is 666 (13:18). What can be made of such references? Surely they must have a symbolical or esoteric meaning.

Still another feature of the Revelation to John, which is characteristic not only of this writing but of other apocalyptic statements as well, will strike the reader as unique. It is the many references to heavenly figures (those not of earth) which appear in this unfolding drama of the end of history. There are the twenty-four elders and the four living creatures around the throne of heaven, already mentioned above (4:4, 6b), "myriads of myriads and thousands of thousands" of angels who sing with a loud voice (5: 11), the Four Horsemen of the Apocalypse (6:1 ff.), a mighty angel who comes down from heaven wrapped in a cloud with a rainbow over his head (10:1), Michael with his fighting angels (12:7), and the great dragon called the devil and Satan (12:9). The references in this section will be interpreted later in this volume when the drama of the Apocalypse itself is considered.

Without going into detail at this point, it is sufficient to indicate that such writing as this is highly symbolical. It employs a kind of code language that was understood by its first readers who lived in a day when apocalyptic expressions were considerably used. The strangeness, uniqueness, or unusual character of such representations belongs to the nature of apocalyptic. Both in the Old Testament scriptures and in noncanonical writings there were precedents for them.[2] Moreover, it is quite likely that the author of the Apocalypse of John actually borrowed from some of these. Beckwith has stated this fact in these words:

> The Book of Daniel, the first great apocalypse, established the norm which later writers followed more or less closely in certain ideas and in forms, symbols, and general structure. Very wide also was the influence in such passages as Isaiah 13-14, Ezekiel 1, 28-39, Joel 2-3, Zechariah 9-14.[3]

In all of this there is a key with which to unlock the mystery of the Apocalypse, a mystery which we have every reason to believe was understood by its original readers.

We must take note, also, that there was a practical consideration behind all apocalyptic that led to the use of cryptic language. These documents were a kind of underground writing intended to encourage believers who were in danger of persecution and to confuse the uninitiated and unfriendly outsider into whose hands they might fall. Many in this century are familiar with publications that were printed under cover by the resistance movements in occupied countries during the war. In a sense, the Apocalypse to John might be regarded as one of these out of the past.

THE PLACE OF VISIONS

Another characteristic of apocalyptic writings that should be noted is that they are frequently, but not always, related to visions

---

[2] Noncanonical apocalypses include Ethiopic Enoch, Slavonic Enoch, the Sibylline Oracles, the Psalms of Solomon, the Odes of Solomon, the Testament of the Twelve Patriarchs, Second Esdras, the Apocalypse of Baruch, *et al*. The recent discovery of the Dead Sea scrolls has brought to light a hitherto unknown noncanonical apocalyptic writing, namely, *The War of the Sons of Light and the Sons of Darkness*.

[3] I. T. Beckwith, *The Apocalypse of John* (New York: The Macmillan Company, 1919), p. 172.

which the author experienced. This is true of the Apocalypse to John. The writer is sometimes referred to as the seer of Patmos in this connection, for at the opening of his drama he says "I was in the Spirit on the Lord's day, and I heard behind me a loud voice like a trumpet saying, 'Write *what you see* in a book' " (1:10-11). Later he states "After this *I looked*, and lo, in heaven an open door!" (4:1), and also "Now *I saw* when the Lamb opened one of the seven seals" (6:1).[4] This same kind of reference appears throughout the book.

A premium was placed upon visions in the first century, more so than in the present. Psychology has made us quite conscious of abnormalities in the mental life, and we have become afraid of them. Having a vision today would send many persons to a psychiatrist. But the Apocalypse was not written in our time. Besides, its author was an Oriental who lived in an environment where the temperament of the people predisposed them to unusual psychical experiences.

We should not hold, however, that a truth based upon a vision is more spiritual, and therefore more authoritative, than one that is founded upon reason. It should be subject to the same tests of validity that we give to ideas that come to us in more usual ways. On the other hand, we should not regard all visions as an evidence of an unstable mental life, as being pathological and illusory. Many saints, Protestant and Catholic alike, have heard God speak through this medium.

From a literary standpoint it is clear that whatever the character of the visions that came to the author of the Apocalypse, in recording them much adaptation took place. There are too many parallels to other apocalyptic writings in both figure and phraseology to be accounted for in terms of a vision alone. This fact has led Martin Rist to write: "The claim made in many apocalypses that the predictions came through visionary experiences is a literary device to give greater impressiveness to these writings." [5] In my own

---

[4] Italics mine.

[5] Martin Rist in *The Interpreter's Bible* (Nashville: Abingdon Press, 1957), XII, 350.

judgment, what we have in the Revelation to John is a series of visions that were later set forth in true apocalyptic vernacular. This would be a reasonable undertaking, and it conforms to the character of the book itself.

COSMOGRAPHY OF THE TIME

We have been considering in these paragraphs the characteristics of apocalyptic literature. In this connection it should be noted that, like all such writings, the Revelation to John reflects the outlook on the natural world that was held at the time of its composition.[6]

This is particularly noticeable in an apocalypse because it usually contains many references to cosmic upheavals and natural calamities. God is represented as using nature in punishing evil men and nations. He employs it freely and is not concerned with what we refer to today as natural law and the uniformity of nature. In one portrayal of the Apocalypse, the moon is turned to blood, stars fall in great showers, and all mountains and islands are removed from their places (6:12-14); yet the universe and life on earth continue to exist. Modern man would find this difficult to fit into his cosmography, or view of the world, but from the outlook of that day this would not have been a problem at all.

There are other references in the book of Revelation which also reveal the beliefs of the author's time regarding the natural world. One of these is the mention of the open door into heaven through which the seer was taken; it was just above the earth (4:1). Again, there is the sky that rolled up like a scroll (6:14). This reflects the then current idea that the heavens were stretched out over the earth like a curtain. We should also take note of the reference to the four angels who stood at the four corners of the earth (7:1), indicating the conviction of the time that the earth was flat. I have personally heard individuals argue against our accepted idea that the earth is round (pear-shaped) on the basis of this text.

Two observations should be made in this regard. First, when the Revelation to John was written, our scientific outlook had not

[6] Cf. the chart on the cosmography of the first century, p. 164.

yet developed. The persons of that day lived, thought, and also had visions in terms of the viewpoint of their own times. Second, there is a real question as to how literally these authors of apocalyptic intended their words to be taken. Although they firmly believed that God would use nature to enforce his will and that he would also use it as an instrument of his judgment, they were describing the events much as a poet would write of the singing of the trees or an artist would paint a purple cow. It was the fact and impression of judgment, rather than a literal portrayal, that was intended. I can quite easily imagine an apocalyptic author saying, "If you prefer that I state it differently, I will give you another picture of calamity, but the message will be just as serious." It was the moral and spiritual meaning that was central and not the package in which it was wrapped.

PSEUDONYMOUS AUTHORSHIP

The final characteristic of apocalyptic writings that we shall mention is that they are almost always pseudonymous, a name other than that of the actual author being attached to them. This time we cannot illustrate this feature by referring to the Revelation to John, since the real author's name is probably mentioned. The words "to his servant John" (1:1) are too specific to imply a pseudonym, as is also the reference to his imprisonment on the island of Patmos (1:9). The actual identity of this "John" is another question, however, to which we shall turn in the next chapter. But that the real author is intended in the references of these opening verses seems likely.

Attaching to a writing the name of another author in place of the real author was done frequently in antiquity. It was intended to give the composition a recognition that the author's own name might not lend to it. Accordingly, early Christian documents were sometimes ascribed to the apostles or other well-known figures in the church. This was not regarded as being the least bit dishonest; it was a customary and accepted practice.

In this chapter we have been considering the nature and interpretation of apocalyptic writing, drawing our illustrations mainly from the Revelation to John. The meaning of an apocalypse, its relation to a particular view of history, its philosophical and psychological roots, and its special characteristics have been briefly examined. We have been impressed with the uniqueness of apocalyptic writing, as well as with its seriousness and significance for the Christian faith. No one can take it lightly when its true nature and purpose are understood.

CHAPTER FOUR

The Setting, Date, and Authorship
of the Revelation to John

In our study thus far we have taken note of the fact that apocalyptic writings lighted the fires of faith in dark times. Desperation and moral conviction as to the goodness of God, under the quickening of the divine Spirit, impelled creative minds to write of the defeat of evil and the victory of righteousness. This is eminently true of the Revelation to John.

A TIME OF PERSECUTION

In general, the setting of the Apocalypse is the Greco-Roman world of the first century when Christians and the Christian church were locked in what appeared to be a death struggle with the pagan political power of Rome. As we shall see later, this power was viewed as being under the control of unseen forces, namely Satan, who worked through his two arch-agents, the imperial Roman authority and the state priesthood. These latter are referred to in the Revelation as the two beasts (13:1 ff., 11 ff.)

By this time the Romans had realized that Christianity was not a Jewish sect and that it did not, therefore, enjoy the privileges of being a "permitted" religion. Accordingly, it was suspect. The air was heavy with persecution, although the book contains few actual descriptions of torture and killing by the ruling powers. It is the tension and the tone of the writing, more than its specific details, that reveal the diabolical pressures of the hour. Yet there are some references to particular suffering and death that leave no doubt as to its existence. Martyrs and martyrdom are in the author's thoughts at all times.

There is a specific reference in the writing to one Christian who had lost his life because of his faith. He is called Antipas and is described as a witness who was faithful (2:13). Beyond the mention of his name we know nothing further about this courageous person. There is also the warning in one of the epistles to the seven churches found in the Apocalypse (2-3). This letter to the church at Smyrna says in no uncertain terms, "the devil is about to throw some of you into prison"; it therefore urges them to be faithful unto death (2:10).

In addition to this, the author of the writing says that he himself had once been a prisoner on the island of Patmos, incarcerated there because of his preaching of the word of God and his testimony to Jesus. Patmos was a rocky promontory, jutting out of the Aegean Sea about ten miles west of Miletus, the port where Paul said farewell to the Ephesian elders on his way to Jerusalem (Acts 20:17 ff.). It was a penal colony where convicted citizens of distinction were imprisoned and compelled to labor in the quarries.

THE REASON FOR THE PERSECUTIONS

We have seen that the Christians to whom the Apocalypse was written were confronted with persecution. This is clearly evident in the writing itself. The reason for this persecution is also given —they refused to worship the emperor. Even though expressed in a somewhat cryptic manner, certain statements of the author quite definitely indicate the nature of the situation that the church was facing.

Chapter thirteen of the Apocalypse is particularly significant in this regard. It presents a picture of enforced emperor worship, a practice that was customary now and again in the Roman world. As was stated earlier, the imperial ruling authority was referred to by the author of the Revelation to John as a beast,[1] as were also the priests—collectively considered—who served him and pro-

---

[1] "It is not the political order as such, . . . it means the imperial world power as a perverted political institution, the cunning ruthless greed of the empire, which absorbs everything that it meets." Hanns Lilje, *The Last Book of the Bible* (Philadelphia: Muhlenberg Press, 1957), p. 189.

moted his worship. Both "beasts" were considered to be under the control of Satan, sometimes known in this writing as the dragon.

With this background in mind the meaning of such words as the following becomes clear:

> **Men worshiped the dragon, for he had given his authority to the beast, and they worshiped the beast, saying, "Who is like the beast, and who can fight against it?"**
>
> —*Rev. 13:4*

But there is more. Our author goes so far as to indicate some of the procedures followed in emperor worship. He describes the priests as they go about their tasks. They set up an image to the emperor, caused smoke or steam to come from its nostrils to simulate breathing, and by the use of ventriloquism made it appear to speak:

> **It [the second beast or imperial priesthood] works great signs, even making fire come down from heaven to earth in the sight of men; . . . bidding them make an image for the beast . . . ; and it was allowed to give breath to the image of the beast so that the image of the beast should even speak, and to cause those who will not worship the image of the beast to be slain.**
>
> —*Rev. 13:13-15*

In order to indicate how emperor worship was enforced, our author states that those who went to the local shrine to practice it were "marked on the right hand or the forehead" (13:16). Ostracism, either social or economic, was shown against them if they did not bear this emblem. Whether the mark was literal—a stamp or tattoo—or simply the kind of thing we have in mind when we say that a person is a "marked man" is not clear. It is suggestive to note that Alexandrian Jews were required by Ptolemy Philadelphus to have the emblem of Dionysius tattooed upon their hands (III

Macc. 2:29). The mark in the Apocalypse, however, may be a mystical one, such as the mark of God that rests on the faithful (7:3). In any case, the worshipers were singled out as being loyal to the emperor, and those who did not participate were regarded as traitors and became objects of persecution and even death.

The purpose of emperor worship was to unify the people of the far-flung Roman world into a single body. As with one heart and deed they expressed their loyalty to the imperial power of the state by scattering incense before the bust of the emperor, they were cementing the joints of the empire into a unified whole. This was particularly needed in the outlying provinces where their great distances from Rome lessened their awareness of belonging. But it was also practiced in the capital city itself with the residence of the emperor close at hand.

The Christians resisted this demand. They would worship no one but Jesus Christ. He alone was Caesar. Did he not have inscribed on his robe and thigh the name "King of kings and Lord of lords" (19:16)? There have been those who have suggested that no great sin would have been involved in performing outwardly the simple act that was required, while inwardly holding mental and spiritual reservations. But so great was their devotion to Christ, and so final was their moral commitment to honesty in daily living, that to dissemble in this fashion was psychologically and ethically impossible for the Christians. They had been taught that yea was *yea* and that nay was *nay*. Deceit was of the devil; in fact he is actually called a deceiver in the Apocalypse (20:3).

EMPEROR WORSHIP AND THE DATE OF THE BOOK

Emperor worship was not just an academic matter; it was too deeply ingrained into the texture of the situation that the Christians were facing at that time to be so regarded. Since the imperial authority of Rome was identified with the power of Satan himself, the issue of whether or not to pay the emperor divine honors became a matter of deciding for good or evil, for love or hate, for heaven or hell, for Christ or the dragon. On which side shall one's life be cast? This was the question the Christians were facing.

The portrayal of emperor worship found in the Apocalypse helps us in dating it. We must find a situation involving this practice in that early time that fits best the picture contained in the book itself. As we consider, therefore, the emperors of the first century A.D. we turn at the outset to Caesar Augustus (27 B.C.-A.D. 14). He was considered by the populace as divine, but he died before the beginning of the Christian church. The book of Revelation could not possibly have been written while he was on the throne. Caligula (37-41), sometimes known as Mad Gaius, also wanted recognition as a god—even to his desire that a bust of himself be placed in the Temple at Jerusalem. This was about as far as it went, since he was killed before he could enforce his own worship. It is unlikely, therefore, that he is the beast.

Nero (54-68) likewise accepted divine honors; moreover, he was a vigorous persecutor of the Christians. But his reason for doing this was not because they refused to worship him; it was due to the fact that he placed upon them the blame for the great fire that nearly consumed the Eternal City. Therefore, the book was probably not written during his reign, although there are several interesting references in the Revelation to his returning to life (13:3, 12, 14; 17:8, 11) that we shall soon examine. Vespasian (69-79) also allowed himself to be worshiped as divine; but he did not promote the practice, and it never developed into a strong cult. In fact, he is supposed to have said on his deathbed—being highly swollen at the time—that he looked rather ridiculous for a god. His period, therefore, is not suitable as a setting for the writing.

THE REIGN OF DOMITIAN

This brings us to the reign of the emperor Domitian (81-96). The record here is enlightening. Not only was he willing to be accorded divine honors, but he also promoted the idea with intense enthusiasm. More than any of the rulers who preceded him in the first century, this monarch made his recognition as a god a deliberate pursuit. There was something pathological in his passion to be worshiped. Some have suggested that it was because for so many years he had found it necessary to live in the shadow of his older brother Titus, who preceded him as Caesar, that he now desired to outshine him. Perhaps so; but all explanations seem inadequate in the presence of such an egoistic mania.

More than anything else it is the fact that Domitian is known *to have required emperor worship* by his subjects that makes him the most likely candidate for the first beast of the Revelation to John. It is this, therefore, that dates the book during his rule. Since this enforcement was particularly marked at the close of his life, a date around A.D. 95-96 for the Apocalypse seems most appropriate.

In compelling his subjects to pay him divine honors, Domitian did not hesitate to employ the Roman army, particularly in the outlying areas of the empire. Banishment, imprisonment, loss of material holdings, and even capital punishment became the lot of those who disobeyed. The royal family itself was not exempt; they too, along with the citizenry, were under the necessity of addressing their kinsman as "our Lord and our God."

DOMITIAN, THE RETURN OF NERO, AND THE IDENTITY
OF THE BEAST

In the previous chapter it was indicated that apocalyptic writings have something in common with the undercover publications that appeared in occupied countries during the war. It was dangerous to indulge openly in contemporary references; yet certain things or persons needed to be pointed out if the papers were actually to communicate and make clear their message. This is true in the case of the Apocalypse to John. The author was under the necessity of identifying the ruling caesar who was oppressing the Christians, but it was also important that he do it in a roundabout fashion. How did he accomplish this?

First of all, in a passage describing the beast he said, among other things, that this evil one had seven heads. And then he added, "One of its heads seemed to have a mortal wound, but its mortal wound was healed, and the whole earth followed the beast with wonder" (13:3). In another place the author wrote of the beast that he "was, and is not, and is to ascend from the bottomless pit and go to perdition" (17:8).

In themselves these verses may seem to say very little; and to make a wild guess as to their meaning would be hazardous. But we are not left in the dark in this situation. We know that there circulated, particularly during the closing years of Domitian's reign, the myth that the emperor Nero was to return from the East with a conquering army. This monarch had died at his own hands under peculiar circumstances, and the idea developed that he had actually risen and was living among the Parthians. It was expected that he would soon return to Rome. Scholars refer to this as the Nero redivivus legend.

When, in attempting to identify the ruling caesar, or the beast, the author of the Revelation to John says that it had *a mortal wound that was healed, and that it was, and is not, and is to ascend,* does this not suggest the Nero redivivus myth we have been relating? And, furthermore, does not the fact that this myth particularly circulated during the latter days of Domitian's rule make it likely that the author was pointing to him as the reappearing Nero? If our answer to these questions is affirmative—which seems reasonable to me—we have here another indication as to the date of the Apocalypse. The ruling monarch was in all probability Domitian.

THE NUMBER 666 AND THE IDENTITY OF THE BEAST

Our author makes yet a further effort to name the beast who exercised Satan's, or the dragon's, authority from the throne at Rome. He does this in the same chapter in which he describes emperor worship. After indicating something of the procedures involved, he adds, quite mysteriously, the words "This calls for wisdom: let him who has understanding reckon the number of the beast, for it is a human number, its number is six hundred and sixty-six" (13:18). There can be no doubt that in this sentence there is a deliberate attempt to identify the beast. It is an open invitation to those who read to decipher the reference.

But how is this to be done? I remember a neighbor who came to our home when I was a boy and excitedly announced to my mother that they had discovered who the beast of "Revelations" (as she put it) really was. It was during World War I and people were turning to the Apocalypse—as they always do in times of stress—for answers to their questions. This friend from the house next door went on to say that the beast was the Kaiser of Germany. Someone had learned that inside his helmet was engraved the number 666. What evidence could be more conclusive than this?

The trouble with such foolish guesses—for that is what they are —is that they violate the very first principle of interpretation in these matters. It is the immediate background to which we must turn for our answers because this was the basis upon which the author wrote and the first readers of the writing read and understood what he had to say.

In that day numbers were sometimes used in relation to the alphabet. Romans, Greeks, and Hebrews alike employed letters as numerical symbols. This is called *gematria*. The alphabetical equivalent in Latin of the figure 666 is *Neron Caesar*. There is a textual variant of this passage which gives the number as 616. The Latin form *Nero Caesar* would lead to this figure. On the surface this would seem to indicate that the author was pointing to Nero as the emperor, thus dating the book in his time. Some scholars accept this conclusion. But in view of the Nero redivivus legend, might not this just as logically suggest that it was Domitian, conceived of as Nero returned, whom the author had in mind? I personally am led to this conclusion, particularly since the picture that the Apocalypse gives of emperor worship also calls for a Domitian date.[2]

The reasons for placing the Revelation to John during the latter part of Domitian's rule that have been suggested in this chapter have been drawn from what the book itself implies.[3] We may call this internal evidence. It is interesting that it is corroborated in a

[2] Cf. the charts at the close of the book for diagrams of attempts to name the person referred to in the number 666. Some of these violate the principle of interpreting the Revelation, first of all, in the light of its immediate background. Pp. 161-63.

[3] For a recent discussion in favor of an early date for the Apocalypse based upon a presumed Aramaic original see Charles C. Torrey, *The Apocalypse of John* (New Haven: Yale University Press, 1958), pp. 58-89.

statement made by the church father Irenaeus (*ca.* A.D. 180), who claimed that the writing "was seen no very long time since, but almost in our day, towards the end of Domitian's reign." [4]

WHO WROTE THE REVELATION?

It has been widely assumed in the popular mind that the author of the Revelation to John was the disciple of Jesus by that name, he who was a brother to James and a son of Zebedee. So general has been this belief that it may appear strange to some that the question of authorship should be argued at all. Besides, this assumption is of long standing. Irenaeus concurred in it as far back as the second century,[5] as did also Justin Martyr (*ca.* A.D. 136).[6] Around A.D. 200, in its list of books accepted as scripture in Rome, the Muratorian Canon likewise says that it was the apostle John who authored it.

Before we decide that this settles the question, we should note that in antiquity there were also those who took issue with the belief that the Revelation was written by John the Apostle. Among these was Marcion (*ca.* A.D. 150), who would have nothing at all to do with it, regarding it as being too Jewish. Another who rejected apostolic authorship was Dionysius of Alexandria (*ca.* A.D. 247-64). He favored John Mark. And the church historian Eusebius (*ca.* A.D. 325) found his candidate in John the Presbyter or Elder. Thus it is clear that there was no uniformity of conclusion among the church fathers as to who wrote the Apocalypse. The external evidence is far from unanimous.

But what does the internal evidence suggest? What do we learn from the book itself as to the identity of the author who wrote it? First of all, we are told by the writer that his name is *John*.[7] He

---

[4] Irenaeus, *Against Heresies*, Book V, ch. 30.3 in *The Ante-Nicene Fathers* (New York: Charles Scribner's Sons, 1905), I, 558. Cf. also Eusebius, *Ecclesiastical History*, Book III, ch. 18 in *Fathers of the Church* (New York: Fathers of the Church, Inc., 1953), XIX, 165.

[5] Irenaeus, *Against Heresies*, II, 22.5; III, 3.4: IV, 20. 11, 30.4; V, 26.1.

[6] Justin Martyr, *Dialogue with Trypho, A Jew*, ch. 81 in *The Ante-Nicene Fathers* (New York: Charles Scribner's Sons, 1905), I, 240.

[7] Cf. the discussion of the pseudonymous character of apocalyptic writings in the previous chapter, p. 50.

calls himself Jesus Christ's *servant* (1:1) and says also that he is a *brother* in Christ of those who are to read his work (1:9). With them he had shared in the tribulation, in the kingdom, and in the patient endurance. He had also been imprisoned because of his witness to Christ. Earlier in the chapter we have already taken note of his incarceration at Patmos. From the standpoint of what he says in the Apocalypse about his personal identity, this is all that we are given.

There are other items of information that the Revelation contains about the kind of person the author is, even though they do not indicate just who he is. For instance, he is one who is readily caught up in the Spirit, sees visions, and reacts deeply. Such expressions as "I was in the Spirit on the Lord's day" (1:10); "I looked, and lo" (4:1); "I saw in the right hand" (5:1); "And I wept much" (5:4); "Then I looked, and I heard" (5:11); "I looked, and behold" (7:9); and "When I saw her I marveled greatly" (17:6) reveal a deeply sensitive person. He is a part of what he sees, hears, and feels.

From the way the author writes, it is a likely conclusion that he is a Jewish Christian. He thinks within the framework of a Jewish background, even to regarding himself as an inspired prophet (19:10; 22:7, 9, 18). On every hand there is evidence that he knew the Hebrew scriptures since, either by quotation, allusion, or overtone, he makes constant use of them throughout the writing. Estimates of the extent of this usage vary from scholar to scholar. Some would seem to be excessive, but there can be little doubt that his own scriptures were always before him. They colored his visions and affected his literary style. Along this same line it has been suggested that the reason his use of Greek was so faulty was that he could not get away from Hebrew thought forms; he thought in Hebrew as he was writing in Greek.

However, for all his Hebraic characteristics, the author of the Revelation was decidedly a Christian. He was evidently well known in the church since he did not introduce himself to his readers beyond the mentioning of his first name. We have already noted that he had suffered because of his witness to Jesus, even though it

61

seems rather evident that he had not seen his Lord in the flesh, and certainly not to the extent of being a personal disciple and close follower of Christ during his ministry. References in the book to Jesus' earthly life are too scant and remote to have been written by a close companion. He shows a feeling for the apostles as would one outside the group (18:20; 21:14). Writing in the middle of the last decade of the first century he looks back reverently, if not realistically, to former days.

A SUMMARY

We have seen that the early church fathers do not agree as to the identity of the author of the Apocalypse. He is regarded by some as the apostle John and by others as John Mark or John the Elder. Modern scholars also differ in their conclusions as to the authorship of the book. Some suggest John the Apostle, some support John the Presbyter or Elder, and some use the general title of John the Seer, for want of a specific name. All of this reveals considerable lack of agreement.

On the other hand, a study of the book itself has proved helpful in approaching the question of authorship. While it does not name him beyond using the one word John, it does indicate many of his characteristics. These characteristics seem to rule out the apostle, but they still leave the decision as to his actual identity open.

Although it would be interesting—and perhaps quite satisfying —to be able to definitely name the author, there is no great loss in withholding judgment. Whatever his full name might be, whoever he was, he still shows himself in his writing to be a Christian of great faith, dauntless courage, penetrating insight, and dramatic creativity. He has shared with men throughout the ages his vision of the ultimate victory of Christ over the forces of evil as has no other in Christian history. Such a one is well known although he remains unnamed.

In this chapter we have considered such questions as the setting, date, and authorship of the Revelation to John. It is quite significant that, although some matters remain unsettled, much may actually be known about these subjects.

THE UNFOLDING DRAMA

CHAPTER FIVE

Preparation for Destiny

In the preceding chapters we have been considering the background of the Revelation to John. How important this is in interpreting the Apocalypse cannot be overemphasized. Not to take it into consideration would make a correct interpretation of the book impossible.

WHAT HAS BEEN LEARNED

Several significant facts have come to the fore. The first is that an apocalyptic writing contains a philosophy of history; it has to do with the outcome of human events as these are related to the purpose and judgment of God. Next, it became apparent that we could not understand the particular approach to history found in the book of Revelation apart from viewing it in relation to the outlook of the Scriptures as a whole in this regard. It must be read within this larger setting or it will appear to be merely a peculiar document; whereas, it is actually a magnificently individualistic one.

In the third place we discovered that the Apocalypse represents a unique type of thinking that expresses itself in a highly stylistical form of writing. And finally we took note of the fact that the book belongs to a particular period in time, that it has a setting in history which must be faced. This involves the situational background, the date, and the authorship. All of this represents a considerable body of knowledge. But there is no writing in the entire Bible where such information is as necessary, if the word of God is to come home to us when we read it, as in the case of the Revelation to John.

PREPARATION FOR DESTINY

This chapter has been titled "Preparation for Destiny." The reason for this is that it will examine that section of the Apocalypse in which the author prepares his readers for the unfolding drama of coming events that he is to present. It was important that they should be properly introduced to what lay ahead for them before they actually faced it. They needed to be made ready for such a startling announcement of destiny—their own, and also that of all mankind.

How does John accomplish this? First, he introduces himself to his readers with a statement of what he is to do (1:1-8). Next, he presents his vision of Jesus Christ as one "like a son of man." This is he who stands as the transcendent authority behind the prophecy of the future and who is the very agent through whom it will be fulfilled (1:9-20).

But more is needed if the accounting is to be realistic. What of conditions on earth where the judgment is to fall? What is the status in heaven from whence it is to descend? The first of these questions is answered in a series of seven letters which the author is commanded to write to seven churches in Asia (2:1-3:22). The second is dramatically considered by a portrayal of perpetual worship before the Divine Presence in the throne room of heaven (4:1-5:14).

THE REVELATION OF JESUS CHRIST

1:1-8

There is no better way to begin the interpretation of the Apocalypse itself than to turn to the author's own words as he opens the writing. With a directness and finality that immediately face his readers with the scope and significance of his undertaking, he says:

> The revelation of Jesus Christ, which God gave him
> to show to his servants what must soon take place; and
> he made it known by sending his angel to his servant

John, who bore witness to the word of God and to the testimony of Jesus Christ, even to all that he saw. Blessed is he who reads aloud the words of the prophecy, and blessed are those who hear, and who keep what is written therein; for the time is near.

—*Rev. 1:1-3*

In these two sentences John states a number of highly important things. His writing is to be a revelation of Jesus Christ, an unveiling of hidden supernatural truth. God is its source. It is intended for Christian believers and has to do with events that are shortly to occur. Thus it involves the first readers themselves; they are to experience and participate in what is to happen. The knowledge of these things was given to John, the servant of Christ, by an angel who symbolizes its heavenly origin. In sharing it, the seer is bearing a personal witness to what he saw. All of this is of such great importance that a promise of blessedness is given to those who read aloud the prophecy, as well as to those who hear it and keep it.

After making these introductory statements, John felt that he should further undergird the revelation he was to make by giving his readers some of the great Christian affirmations concerning Jesus Christ (1:4-7). Phrase spills over phrase in rapid succession as words that have already taken on a special meaning within the church come from the writer's pen. The Lord is the faithful witness, the first-born of the dead, and the ruler of kings on earth. With his blood he has freed men from their sins, making them both a kingdom and priests to God. He is to be praised; glory and dominion are to be his forever and ever, and when he returns to earth on the clouds all will see him. Even those who crucified him will wail in their plight, since judgment will be upon them.

A VISION OF THE SON OF MAN
1:9-20

It is highly appropriate that the Revelation should open its dramatic portrayal of the final destiny of men and nations with the vision of one like a son of man. John says that it came to him

67

while he was in the Spirit, suggesting that he may have been in a trance. Here is to be found the power, the authority, and the grandeur of being that such a one must possess if he is to be the agent of all human destiny. Here also is the source of the author's call to be a prophet, for it was this exalted personage who said to him, "Write what you see in a book." This is reminiscent of the calls of the Old Testament prophets. (Cf. Isa. 6; Jer. 1:1-12.)

Look at the figure of Christ that John describes. He stands "clothed with a long robe and with a golden girdle round his breast" (1:13). Kings wear garments of such dignity, and priests bind girdles about their person as a sign of their special function. His hair is as "white as wool" or "snow," and his burning eyes are as a "flame of fire." This shows him to be a person of divine prestige and penetrating insight (1:14). Was not God, he who was the "ancient of days" to Daniel (7:9), so dressed, and did not the angel who spoke to this prophet in Babylon thus appear (10:6)?

But there is more. The Christ who is as a son of man has feet "like burnished bronze," and when he speaks his voice is like "the sound of many waters" (1:15). This again suggests the angel in Daniel (10:6), and those who first read these words were, even as the author, moved to think of similar heavenly power and authoritative utterance.

The impressiveness of this divine figure lies not in his appearance alone. He has a function to perform, exercising control over the churches since he holds them in his right hand like "seven stars." As such they are dependent upon him; he is their strength and their hope. The wicked, however, will feel the sharp bite of a "two-edged sword" that issues from his mouth, pronouncing judgment and effecting destruction (1:16). One cannot but wonder whether the churches were not reminded by this representation of Isaiah's portrayal of the Messiah who would smite the earth with the rod of his mouth and with the breath of his lips slay the wicked (11:4). In any case it was this very task that Christ was to be seen as performing in the Revelation.

Then John says that Christ's face "was like the sun shining in full strength" (1:16). The Transfiguration may well have been in the seer's mind as he recorded this part of his vision. On the lofty mountain top—probably Mount Hermon—the disciples had witnessed the glorious light of heaven that illumined the being of Jesus. This was but a glimpse of the greater brilliance that was truly his and which he would reveal in his future work as the Messiah.

Little wonder that the seer notes that he fell on his face before the awesome sight of this dazzling figure; for this was "the first and the last," the resurrected Lord who was crucified and rose again to live forever. Death and Hades alike were under his control (1:17-18). The Christ who is portrayed here is equal to history's greatest hour—the hour of her culmination and conclusion.

There are many interesting suggestions in the commentaries regarding the origin, literary and otherwise, of these representations of the divine character of Christ. These should not be missed, even though this matching of symbol with source may sometimes become too rigid and too mechanical. That John the Seer was widely read in the apocalyptic and prophetic literature of his religious heritage—and depended extensively upon it—cannot be doubted. His use of the expression "son of man" bears witness to this fact. As we have already noted in this book, the phrase and the conception it carries has had a long history. Our author, in employing it, has in mind the high signification of a special agent of God that it represents.[1]

Before leaving the vision of the authoritative Christ possessed of heavenly power and majesty with which the Apocalypse opens, one is tempted to inquire how it was that the carpenter-preacher of Galilee came to be thought of in such supernal terms. The answer most probably lies in the experience of the Resurrection and Ascension by the early church. It was here that the true stature of Jesus as the Christ was revealed and finally realized by his followers. And their continuing experience of him as living and exalted Lord further contributed to this insight.

[1] Cf. p. 27.

THE LETTERS TO THE SEVEN CHURCHES
2:1-3:22

Now that John has recorded this impressive vision of Christ as one like unto a son of man, he is ready to turn his attention to conditions on earth where this transcendent figure is to exercise his authority in both blessing and judgment. He does this by depicting the situation in seven Asian churches: Ephesus, Smyrna, Pergamum, Thyatira, Sardis, Philadelphia, and Laodicea.[2] A look at the map will show that they are in the area where Paul's influence extended during his long stay of at least three years in Ephesus (Acts 20:31). The great apostle himself may even have founded some of them, directly or indirectly, as emissaries from his headquarters went forth to proclaim the gospel, or as converts in the large city returned to their home communities to bear their personal testimony.

Some scholars have contended that the seven letters had an earlier and separate existence in varying forms apart from the Apocalypse or that they were a later editorial addition. In language, symbolism, and purpose, however, it seems to me that they belong where they are in the New Testament and were written at the same time as the rest of the book.

There is no reason but to think that these seven were typical of Christian churches elsewhere in the Greco-Roman world. It has even been suggested, with considerable merit, that because the number seven is involved John has in mind the church universal, seven being a figure that symbolizes completeness. This, then, would represent the state of the entire church in that day. Yet the details given, letter by letter, so fit what is known about the communities mentioned, that it is difficult not to conclude that the author is thinking of seven specific situations. We do not need to decide between these two points of view, symbolical writing being what it is. Both may be true at one and the same time.

---

[2] A helpful description of these seven communities in relation to the contents of the seven letters may be found in Thomas S. Kepler, *The Book of Revelation* (New York: Oxford University Press, 1957), pp. 54-73.

In writing to the seven churches, John has followed a specific method. Each communication contains a formal pattern: the one who speaks is mentioned; the church is praised and blamed (either or both); and finally a promise is given "to him who conquers."

Who is the one who speaks in the letters? He is none other than the Christ depicted in the vision of one like unto a son of man. In each communication this identification is made by repeating one of the representations in the vision, such as "the words of him who holds the seven stars in his right hand" (The church at Ephesus, 2:1), "the words of him who has the sharp two-edged sword" (the church at Pergamum, 2:12), "the words of the Son of God, who has eyes like a flame of fire, and whose feet are like burnished bronze" (the church at Thyatira, 2:18).

In spite of this deliberate identification of the speaker with the one who is like unto a son of man, before each letter closes John also states, "He who has an ear, let him hear what *the Spirit* [3] says to the churches" (2:7, 11, 17, 29; 3:6, 13, 22). This is most interesting and significant from the standpoint of New Testament thought and conviction. It implies that it is through the Holy Spirit that Christ speaks to the church. This is characteristic of New Testament experience as a whole and provides a basis for the doctrine of the trinitarian nature of God.[4]

And what does this glorified Christ say to the churches? Four of them (Ephesus, Pergamum, Thyatira, Sardis) are both praised and censured. Two (Smyrna and Philadelphia) receive nothing but unrestrained approval. One (Laodicea) is wholly criticized. Commendations are given for such achievements as patient endurance (Ephesus, 2:2), riches in Christ (Smyrna, 2:9), martyrdom (Pergamum, 2:13), loving and faithful service (Thyatira, 2:19), purity (Sardis, 3:4), and loyalty (Philadelphia, 3:8). Censure is passed upon some for such sins as loss of devotion (Ephesus, 2:4), immorality, particularly in connection with emperor worship (Pergamum, 2:14-15), false teaching and unseemly sexual prac-

---

[3] Italics mine.

[4] For further consideration of similar data the reader may examine such passages as the following: Acts 16:6-7; Rom. 8:9-10; II Cor. 3:17.

tices (Thyatira, 2:20 ff.), spiritual deadness (Sardis, 3:1), and indecisiveness (Laodicea, 3:15-16).

It can be seen that these are the sins of some in the Church in every generation, even as here also are the spiritual achievements in Christ that represent the fruits of the Spirit down through the centuries. It is this fact that makes the letters to the seven churches so meaningful. Every generation can find itself somewhere in these significant communications. Probably no section of scripture has provided a basis for more series of sermons than these brief epistles.

Before concluding this section, some reference should be made to the promises of reward that are given in these letters by the exalted Christ of the Apocalypse. In each case they are said to be reserved for those who conquer or overcome. How appropriate for a time of threat and trial for the churches!

As is typical of apocalyptic writings, these blessings are usually referred to in symbolical fashion. The faithful who remain loyal in the face of terrific temptations are said to be allowed to eat of the tree of life, which is in the paradise of God (Ephesus, 2:7), to escape the final judgment (Smyrna, 2:11), to be given a new and secret name that assures protection and admission to the order of the redeemed (Pergamum, 2:17), and to be granted great power and the morning star, which is Christ himself (Thyatira, 2:26 ff.). The promises continue. The victors in the struggle are to be clad in the white garments of triumph as they walk with Christ, and find their names written in the role of the saved (Sardis, 3:4-5), to be made as a pillar of strength in the temple of God, bearing both the name of God and of his city, the new Jerusalem (Philadelphia, 3:12), and finally, to feast with the Eternal in the kingdom, sharing his very throne (Laodicea, 3:21).

There were never such letters as these. In true symphonic fashion tremendous themes appear and reappear. Ominous warnings provide a dark background for glowing promises. A living church can be seen struggling to be loyal unto death, and a victorious Christ reigns before all, both strong and tender as he watches over his own.

THE HEAVENLY WORSHIP

4:1-5:14

At the beginning of the Apocalypse John was commanded to write concerning what he saw in the visions. It was then indicated that these had to do with "what is and what is to take place hereafter" (1:19). Thus far we have been looking with the author at the first of these, the things that are and which form a basis for the future that shall be. These include the glorified and regnant figure of one like unto a son of man, as well as the Christian church of the first century in its strength and weakness.

There is yet another factor or element in the contemporary situation which must be included—the heavenly realities. To consider these is true realism. When men are urged to be realistic, it is usually an invitation to face cold, hard facts. This is as it should be. Too often, however, these facts as presented are limited to this earth with its time-space order. Heaven, God, and unseen spiritual matters are considered too speculative to be real. It is assumed that one may add them to life if he is temperamentally so inclined, but to include them in everyday reckonings would be visionary and impractical.

Here is where the author of the Revelation would part company with those who hold such a philosophy. Heaven and the world of spirit were as real to him as any physical object. They belonged in any consideration of both the present and the future, for they represented the final reality, spelled with a capital *R*. Unamuno, the distinguished Spanish philosopher, once said that he would know in the very moment after death whether life on earth was good. If there were a heaven worth possessing, it would be so; if not, it would be otherwise. John, however, would say to him that he knows *now* that life is good, for *God is,* and *heaven is also.* All may not be right with the world, but all is under the ultimate control of a righteous God and will finally express the divine purposes of creation. It is just this conviction that the writer of the Apocalypse wishes his readers to grasp in chapters four and five. In view of the storms that are coming, they will need it.

Passengers on a plane who find the flying frightening are re-assured when they catch a glimpse of the confident captain in the cockpit. Even so the readers of the Revelation would be made bold to hold firm in the frantic future if they were enabled to see God the creator on his throne in heaven, and Christ the lamb and redeemer standing before him. This is the purpose of the two chapters now under consideration. They present a vision of heavenly realities intended to strengthen the will, fire the heart, and inspire faith to hold fast.

GOD THE CREATOR

4:1-11

In approaching this vision it is well to recall that it is God himself who is the source of the universe and upon whom all life ultimately depends. Although first-century persons did not hold our outlook regarding the natural world, they did discern this prime truth. It is as basic for us today as it was for them. There-fore it is highly appropriate that the first anthem of praise to be raised to God in the Apocalypse should laud his work as creator.

The vision that is given to John—and which he describes with unusual sensitivity and feeling—takes him to the throne room in heaven where God reigns. All eyes focus upon him who sits on the throne. Yet he himself is not actually pictured. This may reflect the onetime Jewish hesitancy to deal too familiarly with God, even to the point of refusing to pronounce his name. In any event, everything that is delineated is intended to contribute to the impressiveness of his person. It is not to be regarded as literal description, but as indicative of the spiritual realities of the heaven-ly world.

The mention of the precious stones, jasper and carnelian, the noting of the resplendent rainbow that looked like an emerald as it surrounded the throne, and the reference to the twenty-four elders who were clad in white garments and wore crowns as they sat on twenty-four thrones about the throne of God—all these were not included for their own sake but that they might bring out the glorious character of God's being. The impression is heightened by the description of the sea of glass before the throne that reflects this splendor, by the mention of the lightning, the voices, and the peals of thunder that suggest the power and majesty of the Eternal, and by the reference to the seven torches of fire that possibly represent the divine Spirit.

This is not all, however. There were also the four living creatures, probably suggesting the cherubim and seraphim, or possibly symbols of the several orders of creation (man, domestic animals, wild animals, birds). These were grouped around and on each side of the throne and joined the twenty-four elders as they cast their crowns before God in perpetual singing and worship.[5] There were songs upon their lips—songs that may be reminiscent of the earliest Christian hymns:

> Holy, holy, holy, is the Lord God
>   Almighty,
> who was and is and is to come!
>   —*Rev. 4:8*

.   .   .   .

> Worthy art thou, our Lord and
>   God,
>   to receive glory and honor and
>   power,
> for thou didst create all things,
> and by thy will they existed and
>   were created.
>   —*Rev. 4:11*

The point in these "Te Deums" is that God is worthy of the highest praise. He is the creator of all that is. By his own will he called it into being. Therefore, glory, honor, and power belong rightly to him.

[5] It is recommended that the reader should consult the commentaries for a more detailed discussion of the several representations in this vision, and particularly for suggested sources in other writings that carry an implication for their meaning as John uses them. Our own author here, however, should be allowed to be himself and not considered to be a mere copyist.

CHRIST THE REDEEMER
5:1-14

In the Christian life not only are we dependent upon God the creator, but we are also under eternal debt to Christ the redeemer. This, too, is one of the facts of existence ("what is") that concerned John, and it was important that it should be considered before moving into a description of the judgments that were to precede the Final Assize, the end of time, and the coming of the new heaven and the new earth. In fact, in the heavenly preview that was given the seer it was Christ the redeemer who held the key which unlocked the future; he alone could open the seven seals that bound tight the scroll of coming events.

This scene in the author's vision is a continuation of that in which God is praised as creator. The Eternal is portrayed as still seated upon his throne (he will never abdicate), holding in his hands a completely sealed scroll. One is being sought who is worthy to open it. The destiny of mankind is involved; hence, a special One, a worthy One, must be found. Heaven, earth, and the waters under the earth contained no such person. But the Christ, depicted as a majestic Lamb, was worthy!

Why was Christ worthy? It was because he had died to save men from their sins, bringing them such freedom as a ransom will provide for a slave. This is the reason he is seen in the vision as "a Lamb standing, as though it had been slain" (5:6). Note that although it had been killed, the Lamb *is still standing*, standing in omnipotence (it possesses seven horns) and in omniscience (it possesses seven eyes). Do not waste any pity upon the Lamb; the time for that is past. Since the crucifixion on Calvary, the Resurrection and Ascension have established him alongside God, possessing the very attributes of God himself.

In all of his divinity, Christ the Lamb is also seen here as the historic Messiah. He is called the "Lion of the tribe of Judah" and also the "Root of David." It is significant that the messianic hopes of the Hebrews are being fulfilled even in heaven. They were not misled; it was only that their dream of the Messiah was transformed into something far greater than the rule of an earthly Davidic king.

Before the vision closes, divine praise spontaneously breaks forth. Once again the four living creatures sing praises; once more magnificent songs are lifted, this time to laud Christ as redeemer. It is a new song that they sing, universal in its outreach and triumphant in its tone:

> "Worthy art thou to take the scroll
>   and to open its seals,
> for thou wast slain and by thy blood
>   didst ransom men for God
> from every tribe and tongue and
>   people and nation,
> and hast made them a kingdom and
>   priests to our God,
> and they shall reign on earth."
>
> —*Rev. 5:9-10*

This hymn, however, is not the only one to be sung. Angelic choirs join with others throughout the universe in antiphonal singing, praising both God and Christ.

> "Worthy is the Lamb who was slain, to receive power and wealth and wisdom and might and honor and glory and blessing!" [6] And I heard every creature in heaven and on earth and under the earth and in the sea, and all therein, saying, "To him who sits upon the throne and to the Lamb be blessing and honor and glory and might for ever and ever!" And the four living creatures said, "Amen!" and the elders fell down and worshiped.
>
> —*Rev. 5:12-14*

The preparation for destiny has been completed. John the Seer has been introduced and his purpose in writing the Apocalypse explained. Christ, he who is like a son of man, has been presented

---

[6] There are seven tributes mentioned here. This suggests that Christ, the Lamb, is worthy of receiving all the recognition that earth and heaven can give.

as the authority behind the prophecy and as the agent of its fulfillment. Conditions within the earthly church have been described, and the status in heaven of God, his Son, and the heavenly beings has been made known. All is now in readiness for a reading of the future.

CHAPTER SIX

Visions of Judgment

We have seen that the author of the Apocalypse to John has sought to prepare the church for receiving the revelation of the monumental events that will mark the final judgment of mankind, the end of history, and the establishing of a new order of life for the blessed in Christ. He has done this by introducing himself and his message and by presenting a vision of the Christ who is the authority behind the book, as well as the agent of its fulfillment. Finally, he gave a picture of conditions within the church on earth, followed by a portrayal of the situation in heaven, where God and the Lamb preside with power and authority in the midst of magnificent choral praises. He is now ready to reveal the future to those who are desperately in need of courage and consolation as they face struggle, persecution, and death.

AN OUTLINE OF THE FUTURE

It is at this point that an outline of the rest of the Apocalypse will prove helpful in following the main thread in this unfolding drama. Because of the nature of apocalyptic writings in general and the style of the author in particular, it is easy to lose one's way. This need not happen, however. John's design of procedure may be grasped so that we shall find ourselves moving from point to point with a sense of direction, increasing interest, and mounting anticipation.

TWO SUGGESTED OUTLINES

In considering an outline it must be remembered that the author of the Revelation did not give us one himself, except as he wrote his book in a certain way and according to a definite pattern.[1] The outline must be abstracted from the writing by the person who is putting it down on paper. All that can be claimed for it, then, is that it approximates what John had in mind. This also accounts for the variations among the several outlines one finds in the different books or commentaries.

A typical outline may be found in John Wick Bowman's volume, *The Drama of the Book of Revelation*.[2] It divides the Apocalypse into a sequence of seven major visions. Several scenes are listed under each of these. As we have seen, the seer frequently employs the number seven throughout the Apocalypse, and this fact suggests that we look for it in any attempt to discover an outline within his material. The seven visions, their titles, and the textual divisions follow; the subordinate scenes are omitted here so that the over-all movement of events might be more immediately discerned:

Prologue
(1:7-8)

Act   I   Vision of the Church on Earth—the Son of Man in Its Midst
              (1:9–3:22)
                   (The Letters to the Seven Churches)

Act   II   Vision of God in Heaven—God's Purpose in History (4:1–8:1)
                   (The Opening of the Seven Seals)

Act   III   Vision of the Seven Angels of the Presence—the Church in
              Tribulation (8:2–11:18)
                   (The Sounding of the Seven Trumpets)

Act   IV   Vision of the Church Triumphant—the Drama of Salvation
              (11:19–14:20; 15:2-4)
                   (The Showing of the Seven Pageants)

---

[1] Our assumption here is that, in general, the book as we have it is a unity, and that, whatever materials from different sources it may contain, a single mind has put it into form. An excellent discussion of the unity of the Apocalypse may be found in I. T. Beckwith, *op. cit.*, pp. 216 ff.

[2] Pp. 15-16. Copyright 1955 by W. L. Jenkins, The Westminster Press, and used by permission.

Act   V   Vision of the Seven Angels of God's Wrath—the World in Agony (15:1, 5–16:21)
            (The Pouring Out of the Seven Bowls)

Act VI   Vision of Babylon's Overthrow—the Drama of Judgment (17:1–20:3; 20:7-10)
            (The Unfolding of the Seven Plagues)

Act VII   Vision of the Church in the Millennium—Consummation of God's Purpose (20:4-6; 20:11–22:5)
            (The Fulfilling of God's Sevenfold Plan)

Epilogue
(22:6-20)

Another, and somewhat different, outline of the Revelation is that given by Ernst Lohmeyer (*Die Offenbarung des Johannes*) and presented in English by Martin Rist in *The Interpreter's Bible*.[3] Here also it is discovered that John employs the number seven as a basic figure in structuring his writing. After indicating some introductory material, Lohmeyer lists seven major vision series of seven visions each. It is noted, then, that the book concludes with a supplementary section and an epilogue. The seven major vision groupings are these:[4]

1. Seven Seal Visions 6:1–8:6.
2. Seven Trumpet Woes 8:7–11:19.
3. Seven Visions of the Dragon's Kingdom 12:1–13:18.
4. Seven Visions of Worshipers of the Lamb and Worshipers of the Beast 14:1-20.
5. Seven Visions of the Bowls of God's Wrath 15:1–16:21.
6. Seven Visions of the Fall of "Babylon" or Rome 17:1–19:10.
7. Seven Visions of the End of Satan's Evil Age and the Beginning of God's Righteous Age 19:11–21:8.

With the background that the reader has gained in following the present volume up to this point, these outlines should begin

[3] Martin Rist in *The Interpreter's Bible, op. cit.,* pp. 360-62.
[4] Again I have omitted the detailed listings of the outline for the same reason as previously given.

to take on considerable meaning. We have already been introduced to the Lamb, the dragon, and the beasts. We have become acquainted with the fact that the final consummation of history involves the overthrow of evil and the enthronement of Christ in a new and blessed age.

Other outlines could be presented here. They would be similar to the two that have been given, but would vary in wording and arrangement. All such attempts are prepared and offered as suggestive rather than final. No scholar would claim that any certain outline in all its detail was in John's mind exactly as he deduced it from the seer's book.

THE PLACE OF JUDGMENT IN THE APOCALYPSE

In the passages covered by the suggested outlines three types of material predominate. The first is concerned with visions of judgment, the second with visions of interpretation and explanation, and the third with visions of hope and encouragement. These intermingle throughout the Apocalypse. It is to the visions of judgment that we shall turn in this chapter, and to the others in the two following chapters. The word "judgment" is used in this immediate discussion to refer to acts of judgment involving suffering and punishment for evil. The word may also be employed in connection with the passing of a sentence.

Although it may not always seem to be so, for all their stark tragedy the passages dealing with judgment are also intended to strengthen the Christians who first read the book. It is not that they are to delight in the prospect of the indescribable suffering that is to come upon the wicked; rather, they are to see in these divine acts evidence that righteousness shall ultimately prevail. Christ will be shown to be Caesar, and not the beast who was at present in the seat of imperial power. It was important to know this.

The need for a confirmation of one's faith has been felt through the ages. It is one with the philosopher's continuing quest concerning the nature of the universe: is it essentially good or evil? The search for an answer is apt to be strenuous; and surely in the Apocalypse the answer, when it comes, is costly. Lines must be drawn; issues must come to a head; sides must be chosen; the sheep must be separated from the goats. Although our Christian sensitivity may recoil from this prospect, in a moral universe there is no other alternative except a soft sentimentality that will not do.

As we turn to consider the judgments of the Revelation, it is very important that this truth should be faced. Our entire evaluation of the book is involved in the perspective within which we read and interpret these passages. The inevitability of judgment in a moral universe is a basic truth. It is as realistic to accept it as it is to take seriously the love of God. Men make their choices, and these choices bring certain results. Jesus referred to them as fruits.

Grace and mercy should never be set off in opposition to judgment; they are not antagonistic to each other, but are part and parcel of the same fact. God is righteous; men are created to be righteous; deliberate sin must either be forgiven or punished; the universe is put together in this fashion; there is no escape. It is this philosophy that underlies the judgments of the book of Revelation.

There is yet another element in this picture that must be noted as a background of the judgments in the Apocalypse. It has already been touched upon in connection with our discussion of the dragon and the two beasts.[5] Behind the struggle of the individual man as he chooses between righteousness and evil, the author, true to his times, envisions a cosmic battle that is constantly taking place between the spirit forces of evil and the spirit forces of good. This dualism probably goes back to Persian thought patterns that have been adapted to Christian apocalypticism. On the one side we find God, his son Jesus Christ, the Spirit, and the holy angels; on the other, Satan (the dragon), his agents, the two beasts (symbolizing the Antichrist), and myriads of evil spirits. Men must decide between these opposing powers; accordingly, they will ultimately bear the mark of one or the other. This fact will determine their eternal destiny in the hour of judgment.

[5] Cf. pp. 53-60.

THE THREEFOLD JUDGMENT

Seals, 6; 8:1-6.

Trumpets, 8:7-12; 9; 11:15-19.

Bowls, 15:1-16:21.

Prominent in the developing drama of the Revelation is the threefold judgment of the seven seals, the seven trumpets, and the seven bowls. They are of such great significance and are so typical of the method and message of the writing that I have singled them out for special consideration. In order to have them before us as we consider them, the following outline has been prepared. As each seal is broken, as each trumpet is blown, and as each bowl of God's wrath is emptied, certain actions occur. These are indicated below:

VII SEALS	VII TRUMPETS [6]	VII BOWLS [7]
1. White horse appears bringing conquest. 6:2	1. Hail, fire mixed with blood fall, one third *of earth* burned, etc. 8:7	1. Foul sores come upon those *of earth* who bore mark of the beast. 16:2
2. Red horse appears bringing civil war. 6:3-4	2. Burning mountain thrown into the *sea;* one third becomes blood. 8:8-9	2. *Sea* becomes blood. 16:3
3. Black horse appears bringing famine. 6:5-6	3. Star drops from heaven; *waters of earth* polluted. 8:10-11	3. *Waters* in rivers and fountains become blood. 16:4-7
4. Pale horse appears bringing pestilence. 6:7-8	4. *Heavens* devastated; one third of sun and moon struck. 8:12-13	4. *Sun* scorches men with fire. 16:8-9

VII SEALS	VII TRUMPETS [6]	VII BOWLS [7]
5. Saints under the altar assured. 6:9-11	5. Plague of locusts arises to *torture* five months. The first woe. 9:1-12	5. Kingdom of the beast wreathed in darkness; *anguish, suffering.* 16:10-11
6. E a r t h q u a k e strikes, stars fall, sky vanishes. 6:12-17	6. Four angels released *at the Euphrates.* One third of mankind killed. The second woe. 9:13 ff.	6. River *Euphrates* dried up; three foul spirits released to assemble force for Armageddon. 16:12-16
7. Silence in heaven; series of the seven trumpets begins. 8:1-5	7. Announcement of final *v i c t o r y* made. The third woe. 11:15 ff.	7. Announcement of *victory* made. 16:17-21

How shall this threefold judgment be interpreted? What is its purpose? Does it bear a relationship to the final judgment and consummation of history? Such are the questions that come to our minds as we read these sections of the Revelation.

First you will note that the three series have been referred to here as a single threefold judgment rather than as three separate judgments that occur in sequence. They have been compared to three volleys that come from a single Roman candle, each more brilliant than the other—separate, but fired by one act. Again, they may be likened to a circular staircase having three spirals, each of which is one plane above the others, yet belonging to a single ascending structure. Martin Kiddle's words here are to the point:

[6] To add interest and mystery to the judgment series, John further separates the last three of the trumpets set by designating them the first, second, and third woes (Cf. (9:1 ff.; 9:13 ff.; 11:15 ff.). These seem to grow in intensity (as they move from one to another.

[7] Note the parallels between the trumpet series and the bowl series. Italics have been used to indicate these.

All three accounts cover substantially the same ground, containing information which is often similar, and sometimes almost identical, and ending at the point where the rule of this world ends and the rule of God begins. But each of these series of predictions—the 'seals,' 'trumpets,' and 'bowls' series—has its own individual theme. The last days are described from three different points of view.[8]

A literal reading of these representations, in which they are interpreted as referring to three separate series that occur consecutively, is filled with problems. For instance, at the opening of the sixth seal the sky vanishes (6:14); yet, the blowing of the third and fourth trumpets (8:10-12) presupposes that the sky is still intact, as does also the emptying of the fourth bowl (16:8-9). The answer to such difficulties lies in the nature of apocalyptic writings themselves. They are figurative and imaginative; it is too much to expect them to be logical and consistent at every point. *The fact of judgment, and not the act as described, is central.* Then, too, the three series probably stand for a single brief but sufficient and adequate action, just as the three-and-a-half days the two witnesses lay in the streets in the Apocalypse suggests a brief, incomplete one (cf. 11:9, 11).

THE PURPOSE OF THE THREEFOLD JUDGMENT

It is clear from a reading of the book of Revelation that the threefold judgment series is not the final judgment that attends the end of history. In the first place the destruction and havoc are but partial. Again and again the author says that only one third of life was touched, whether it be the earth, the heavens, the sea, or mankind. In the second place, John, later in his writing, presents the battle of Armageddon where the final death struggle between the forces of good and evil with the attendant carnage occurs, with Christ emerging as the victor (19:17-21. Cf. also 16:16.). All who oppose him are ultimately confined to the lake of fire (20:14-15). At this time judgment is passed upon them according to their record in the book of life.

[8] Martin Kiddle, *The Revelation of St. John* (New York: Harper & Brothers, 1940), pp. 128-29.

Since the threefold judgment that we are examining in this chapter is not final, what is its purpose? Is it a warning to the wicked? Does it contain a call to repentance? Is its purpose disciplinary? The answer to each of these questions must be "No." We may wish that it were otherwise, that through such suffering and in the face of such natural calamities men might re-examine their lives, repent, seek forgiveness, and change their way of living. Not so!

Lest this should shock us with its seeming heartlessness, it must be said that we are here standing at the outer edge of the end of time. As I have written elsewhere, "The perspective of the writing places it at the very yonder-edge of history. The gospel of love has been presented over and over again; presented and rejected. Christ has already died for sinners." [9] Now it would seem to be too late to repent.

If the threefold judgment, then, is not to be an incentive to repentance, what is it intended to accomplish? Its purpose is to soften up society for the final judgment, to prepare it for the great assize. Evil has matured beyond the stage of repentance; it has reached what we sometimes call the point of no return. The time for evangelization has passed.

We do not like to read such words, and there have been those who have rebelled against the Apocalypse's message in this regard, believing that there is always hope of repentance up to the very moment of the final judgment. Does not the shepherd look for the lost sheep *until he finds it* in Jesus' parable? Yes, he does. But our Lord is also said to have spoken of a sin against the Holy Spirit that cannot be forgiven. It is not that God has ceased to be loving but that men, through a continuous, deliberate, and knowing choice of evil, have lost the ability to repent. They no longer can distinguish between good and evil. Dark words, these, to describe an even darker fact.

It should never be forgotten that the Revelation was written primarily for those already within the fold of the church. Its pur-

[9] Charles M. Laymon, *Christ in the New Testament* (Nashville: Abingdon Press, 1958), p. 206.

pose was not so much to convert sinners on the outside as it was to strengthen those who were being persecuted within the Christian community. Since the world did not come to an end at that very time, it has been used quite logically and properly ever since to dramatize the results of evil, to warn sinners, and to inspire repentance and faith. But this was not its original intent.

THE CHARACTER OF THE THREEFOLD JUDGMENT

When one examines in detail the separate parts of the threefold judgment, certain things become evident. The first is the place of nature in these mighty acts of God. Most frequently the heavens are involved: the moon turns to blood (6:12), the stars fall (6:13), the sky disappears (6:14), hail and fire mixed with blood descend upon the earth (8:7), and the sun scorches with a fierce heat (16:9).

Natural elements below the heavens also participate in contributing to the misery: a mountain burning with fire is cast into the sea, causing a third of it to become blood (8:8-9), an army of locusts brings torture and suffering (9:1 ff.), while rivers and fountains become blood (16:4). There is famine (6:5-6), and such pestilence as leads to death (6:7-8). In addition there is conquest (6:2) and civil war (6:3-4). These latter are due to supernatural agencies rather than to the quarrels and differences that develop between peoples and nations. God is using both the natural and supernatural forces he has created to bring judgment upon mankind.

In all of this it should be noted that these eruptions in nature are deliberately caused. They are not regarded as natural calamities that occur normally in the course of events. Instead, they are purposely initiated by God. It is when Christ opens the seals and the angels blow their trumpets or empty their bowls that they take place. We do not have a mechanical view of the natural order in the book of Revelation. God created the universe and God also freely uses the universe for moral purposes.

It should likewise be realized that these acts of judgment involving nature are directed against evil men. This is asserted again and again. Because of the coming of the red horse with its rider (war), peace is taken from the earth and men slay one another (6:4). When the mountains and islands are removed from their places "the kings of the earth and the great men and the generals, and the rich and the strong, and every one, slave and free" hide in the caves as they are stricken with terror and fear (6:14-15). Men die because the waters become wormwood with the falling of the great star from heaven (8:11), and the army of locusts turns from its natural taste for vegetation to torture men, instead, so that they long for death (9:4-6).

With our scientific outlook on the natural world today, we not only have a different conception of the structure of the universe (cosmography) than that held in the time of the writing of the Apocalypse, but we also tend to think of nature as existing in its own right, apart from man.[10] To do otherwise we feel would be anthropomorphic and even childish. But do we not err grievously in the latter conclusion? The biblical conception of the origin of all things as found in the first chapter of Genesis asserts that man was made as the crown of creation. It also implies that the universe was brought into being to provide an environment for his development and growth. This is what John the Seer is reporting in connection with the threefold judgment, only he is saying that on occasion the natural world which ordinarily nourishes man may, when it is called for, also be used by its Creator to judge and punish him.

THE SOURCE OF THE THREEFOLD JUDGMENT

Whence came the vision of the threefold judgment? What is its source? The seer writes that he saw and heard these things. This would imply a vision, or a series of them, on his part. That he actually knew visionary experiences prior to writing the Apocalypse seems to me assured.

But there is more to it than this—far more. John is a literary artist as well as a seer. He does not hesitate to dip his pen into the

[10] Cf. the chart at the close of this volume that depicts the cosmography of the time, p. 164.

writings of the past as he lays before his readers a picture of things to come. We have already indicated that the commentaries should be used in considering the possible background of the multiple representations in the book of Revelation, since it is not within the scope of this book to do this. Some of the suggestions offered may immediately commend themselves as logical and, therefore, likely. Others may seem remote. In any case, it is a sound procedure to approach the book in this fashion.

The threefold judgment lends itself particularly well to this type of analysis. Without going into too much detail it can be easily shown how the broad outline of the representations have their roots in the Old Testament scriptures. For illustrative purposes let us turn, then, to one section of the judgment, to the vision of the Four Horsemen of the Apocalypse.

THE FOUR HORSEMEN OF THE APOCALYPSE
6:1-8

The opening of the first four seals brings four supernatural horses upon the stage of history, one by one. Each has a suggestive color and each a rider. In order, they are white, bright red, black, and pale (livid?). As might be expected, each represents a particular type of calamity associated with war that is to come upon the earth. Traditionally they have been referred to by such titles as conquest, war, famine, and pestilence. Not only does the color suggest these calamities, but also the descriptions of the function of each horse and its rider indicate such activity.

There is a bow, a crown, and one who goes out to conquer when the *white horse* and its rider appear (6:2). The *bright red horse* and he who sits upon it, and to whom a great sword is given, are said to "take peace from the earth so that men should slay one another" (6:3-4). The rider of the *black horse* carries a balance in his hand, one that is used to weigh grain; but how costly it is said to be! Only in time of famine would a quart of wheat and three quarts of barley cost the price of a day's labor, about twenty cents each (6:5-6). The rider of the *pale horse* bears the name of Death, while Hades follows in his train. He kills "with the sword and with famine and with pestilence and by wild beasts of the earth" (6:7-8).

So much for the description of the four horses, their riders, and their missions. Where did John get these ideas, and how did they come to be pictured in this fashion? As we have said previously, it would be natural to conclude that they came to him "out of the blue." In a visionary experience he *saw* and *heard* these things. In fact, John says that this is what happened. Nevertheless, before we conclude too hastily that this is the full story, we should call to mind the fact that apocalyptic writers sometimes "wrote up" their religious convictions using the vision-form to add to their vividness and to enable their readers to visualize their ideas. Even when they had actually seen a vision, as I think our author frequently did, they expressed it in writing by using traditional apocalyptic language.

In the case of the Four Horsemen of the Apocalypse, the use of this process can be convincingly demonstrated. The Old Testament writing, Zechariah, contains two passages that are strikingly similar to John's description in the Revelation. They are Zechariah 1:7-17 and 6:1-8. The first passage pictures four different-colored horses and their riders who move across the earth when God orders it. The prophet sees them in relation to the return of the Jews from captivity in Babylon. The second passage pictures four chariots, symbolical perhaps of the traditional four winds. Interestingly, to each of these chariots horses of various colors are harnessed. The first are red; the second are black; the third are white; and the fourth are dapple-gray. Their function is to bring judgment upon pagan countries or nations.

How like the four horsemen of John these are! There are differences, to be sure, as the seer's creative touch paints the picture; but there can be little doubt but that our author had the Zechariah representations before his mind as he wrote. He would have felt that this gave an added authority to his statement as he adapted them to Christian usage, since the prophet before him had been similarly inspired. For a background to the trumpet and bowl series, the reader may turn to the account of Moses and the plagues in Egypt (cf. Exod. 7:14-25; 9:13-19; 10:4-15, 21-23; 9:8-11; 12:12-20).

In all of this it should not be forgotten that John the Seer is a creative artist as well as a creative personal spirit. The two do not always go together; there are those who feel deeply and whose sensitivities are marked but who cannot communicate to others what they experience themselves. Fortunately John can do both.

We have been considering in this chapter the place of judgment in the book of Revelation. We have found it to be an expression of the righteousness of God in a moral universe. In this particular case, since the action occurs at the end of history, the time for man's repentance and forgiveness is past—it is too late. Nature becomes an instrument of judgment; at the same time supernatural forces are also at work. In describing the coming judgment, the seer brings together both his own visionary experiences and the portrayals in other apocalyptic writings, particularly certain sections of the Old Testament. Our attention was focused primarily upon the preliminary threefold judgment; the final judgment is yet to be considered.

CHAPTER SEVEN

Visions of Interpretation and Explanation

In the previous chapter we were considering the place of judgment in the Apocalypse. It plays a solemn and awesome role in the acts that attend the end of the age. The rigorous character of righteousness is seen in the relentless moving of events toward the Final Assize. Refusal to enthrone Christ in preference to Satan brings suffering beyond belief. All nature is involved; the universe is convulsed in the judging of mankind. It is dreadfully sobering to contemplate the issue between Christ and the dragon as it reaches the hour of its denouement.

Everything, however, is not dark in John's portrayal. The persecuted saints who first read his writing were comforted as well as shocked by the revelations of the seer. All is not unrelieved tragedy; there is also hope and encouragement. As much creative care is given to bring consolation to the church by showing the blessings of the future as is expressed in depicting its judgments. Visions of victory for the faithful are combined with visions of suffering for the wicked.

THE SEER'S OWN LOGIC

Most present-day writers, in picturing such a series of coming events as we have in the Apocalypse, would present a steadily moving development in which scene would follow scene in mounting progression. Each section would take the reader one step further along the way, bringing him nearer to the final crisis. But this is not the seer's way; he has a logic all his own as he arranges his material and tells his story. Unless this logic is understood, much confusion awaits the eager but uninformed reader of the Revelation.

93

What is this logic? Quite simply, it is the alternation of pictures of judgment and pictures of explanation, hope, and encouragement. Just when the reader is ready to be carried along to the next step in the course of the judgments he is, sometimes, brought face to face with a scene that seems unrelated to what has preceded, and which fails to move forward. For a moment he feels stymied and confused. But when it is called to his attention that the author has interrupted his portrayal of the flow of coming events with an interlude that has a purpose all its own, the frustration gives way to understanding and appreciation.

What is the purpose of these interludes, of which there are many? Some are intended to bring understanding, to answer questions in the minds of the faithful. A friend of mine once said that it was not only helpful to know *what* lay beyond the next turn in the road, but also *why*. It is the "why" that John is seeking to present in some of these interludes. Why the judgment? Why the end of the age? Why the drawing of the lines? Why the suffering of the church? Why the experience of the seer himself? These are legitimate questions, and the questioners have a right to seek an answer.

The interludes meet another basic need that the church felt deeply. Encouragement was called for, as well as understanding. The judgments seem so all-encompassing and tragic that even the believers in Christ might be tempted to despair. They needed reassurance, something to increase their morale. And so the seer provides it with a vision of blessed comfort. It should not be hastily concluded that this need for strength is a sign of weakness. The prospect of judgment is terrifying, as the universe itself is envisioned as falling apart. The outlook is explosive in the extreme, and both courage and confidence are needed.

There is yet another purpose behind some of the interludes. It might seem to be a personal one for the author, and yet it is related to the function Christ called upon him to perform. He is terrifically interested in making his point in the Apocalypse. This is no vanity volume; it was not undertaken for fame or fortune. The church desperately needs help and John desperately wants to give it. Any writing technic, therefore, that will assure an eager reading of his book is in order—and presenting the interludes is a part of such a technic. They hold the interest of the reader whose questions they answer, and they create a suspense that makes him eager to read further. In addition, they prepare his mind and spirit for the next stage in the unfolding drama of the end of the age.

Following the first two series (the seals and trumpets) in the threefold judgment, we would expect at the close of chapter nine immediately to find the third series, that of the bowls. Not so! We must wait until the beginning of chapter sixteen in the Revelation to read of this judgment. There are six chapters between the second and third series that interrupt the ongoing development. These contain explanatory and interpretative, as well as encouraging visions of the type we have just been discussing. We have called them interludes. Some writers use the term proleptic visions, since many of them speak of a future event as though it has already taken place. Others refer to them as parentheses, preludes, and intrusions. It is our intention to examine some of these briefly so that their nature and purpose will be understood.

HOW LONG? HOW LONG?
6:9-11

Martyrs and martyrdom were of deep concern to the Christians in John's day, and well they may have been in the face of the historical realities that confronted them. Where were those who had already lost their lives in the struggle with the dragon and his two beasts? The opening of the fifth seal provides the answer to this question:

> When he opened the fifth seal, I saw under the altar the souls of those who had been slain for the word of God and for the witness they had borne; they cried out with a loud voice, "O Sovereign Lord, holy and true, how long before thou wilt judge and avenge our blood on those who dwell upon the earth?" Then they were each given a white robe and told to rest a little longer,

until the number of their fellow servants and their brethren should be complete, who were to be killed as they themselves had been.

—Rev. 6:9-11

There is real poignancy and beauty in this vision. How wonderfully it answers the question concerning the status of those already martyred! They are in the safekeeping of God; in fact, they are under the very altar of heaven—the best of all possible places to be in these circumstances. Here they are patiently to wait until the number of martyrs that is predestined shall be completed. This latter is a reflection of traditional apocalyptic belief that the end would not come until a certain number of martyrs shall have been killed. But I would raise a question, in view of our author's customary handling of traditional ideas and figures, as to whether he intended for this to be interpreted with mechanistic exactness. Yet he did most surely hold that in the economy of history as it moved toward destiny, martyrs made a difference in the outcome.

There is one aspect to this vision that gives us pause. It is the cry of the martyrs, "How long before thou wilt judge and avenge our blood on those who dwell upon the earth?" This seems so unlike the prayers of Jesus and Stephen that their murderers be forgiven. But the times were hazardous, and nerves were on edge. It is possible that this accounts for the seeming spirit of vengeance in the petition of the martyrs. On the other hand, the real meaning of these words may be "how long before this dreadful persecution shall be at an end?" Yet it must be admitted that in their present form they are difficult.

But the response of heaven is not difficult. Each martyr is given a *white* robe. This is the celestial color for special groups. In the Apocalypse angels (cf. I Enoch 71:1) and martyrs on conquering charges (Rev. 19:14) are garbed in white. Even the horses themselves are of this color. You will recall that in the Letters to the Seven Churches, those who overcame were promised that they should be clothed in white garments (3:4-5). It is the color both of purity and victory.

The need of the martyrs for this advance installment upon final blessedness is touching. How human are the greatest of the great! We sometimes elevate the saints of earth too far above their fellow men. They are quite like the rest of their brothers on earth; in their need for reassurance, they are one with us when the darkness of night threatens to engulf our spirits. God knows this and stoops to our weakness. We may assume that the martyrs under the altar were quieted—at least for a time.

WHAT OF THE SEER'S PERSONAL INVOLVEMENT?

10:8-11

One of the questions that would come to the faithful as they sought to remain loyal during these difficult days before the end of history and the coming of the final glory had to do with the experience of the seer himself. Men usually associate the message with the messenger, and in John's case there was no exception to this tendency. So much depended upon him personally, since it was through him that the revelations came. What of his own situation in this picture?

In chapter ten we are given a vision of a mighty angel who came "down from heaven, wrapped in a cloud, with a rainbow over his head." His face was "like the sun, and his legs like pillars of fire" (10:1). He had a little scroll in his hand, and he stood with his right foot on the sea and his left foot on the land. The revelation it contained was for Christians throughout the whole world.

The seer was commanded to "eat" the scroll, to take it into his very own life (10:9). He was personally involved in the events that he was to make known. He could not disassociate himself from them; he would receive no special deliverance. Personal pain and suffering would be his, for the scroll would be "bitter to his stomach." Like the prophets of old, he would experience the desolation of which he spoke. We are reminded of Jeremiah, who knew the suffering that attended the fall of Jerusalem which he had announced.

But all was not to be painful since the scroll was "sweet as honey" in his mouth (10:10). It is an incomparable experience to be a prophet of the Lord. The sweetness of this association is like no other which earth can give. How close to the Divine! How intimate! How awesomely tender! John knew and would yet know the beauty of such a fellowship. Was he not reminded of Jesus who spoke of his own particular kind of joy on the last night of his life as he was already caught up in the suffering of the Cross (John 15:11)?

HOW CAME THE STRUGGLE ON EARTH?

12:7-12

Another question that plagued the faithful had to do with the source of their difficulties on earth. How was it that things came to be as they were? The vision of Michael's war in heaven and Satan's expulsion attempts to answer this and other related questions. Within the framework of a world view that owed much of its origin to Persian thought but had already been absorbed into the Hebrew outlook, John seeks to explain the current tragedy that was besetting the church.

God himself was active in the holocaust that had fallen upon the saints. One of his own archangels, Michael, who had already supported the cause of the Jews against the prince of the kingdom of Persia (Dan. 10:10-17), was involved in its very inception.[1] With his angels he had stormed the ramparts in one of the lower heavens, (the second? fifth?) where Satan's abode was located (cf. Luke 10:18; Eph. 2:2). Satan with his host had been overcome and cast to earth. This prince of evil, also referred to here as the dragon and the devil, was infuriated over his defeat. His wrath was great because he knew that his time was short (12:12). Therefore he was particularly energetic in his persecution of the people of God, those who constituted the new Israel in Christ.

---

[1] Michael is one of the few named angels. Among this group are also Gabriel, Phanuel, and Raphael. The apocalyptic writing among the Dead Sea Scrolls, *The War of the Sons of Light and the Sons of Darkness*, XVII (as found in *The Dead Sea Scriptures*, tr. Theodor Gaster [Garden City, N.Y.: Doubleday & Company, Inc., 1956], p. 304), represents God as using Michael to aid the redeemed: "He [God] will send perpetual help to those who have a share in His redemption through the power of Michael, the mighty, ministering angel."

But he would not win! Heaven had already foreseen the victory over Satan and rejoiced with a loud proclamation, saying,

> Now the salvation and the power and the kingdom of our God and the authority of his Christ have come, for the accuser of our brethren has been thrown down, who accuses them day and night before our God. And they have conquered him by the blood of the Lamb and by the word of their testimony, for they loved not their lives even unto death. Rejoice then, O heaven and you that dwell therein! But woe to you, O earth and sea, for the devil has come down to you in great wrath, because he knows that his time is short!
>
> —*Rev. 12:10-12*

This outburst in heaven expressed full confidence that the faithful, who are called "our brethren," would conquer. The means of their expected victory are the blood of the Lamb and the word of their own testimony. Christ and they together, neither of whom "loved not their lives even unto death," would win out in the end.

This passage in the Revelation is unique in that it not only explains the source of the struggle but also encourages the church by foreseeing its victory. Heaven believes in the followers of the Lamb. Together with Christ they are unassailable.

WHO ARE SATAN'S AGENTS AMONG MEN?
13:1 ff.

In the previous vision the seer sought to explain the struggle of the saints on earth in terms of an event in heaven—Michael's war and Satan's expulsion. There was more here than could be accounted for on purely humanistic grounds. The so-called accidents of history—involving political, sociological, economic, and psychological forces—were too ineffectual to have caused it. Only a heavenly event provided a sufficient explanation; Michael had cast out Satan.

The battle, therefore, has now been moved from heaven to earth. It is here that Satan (the dragon and devil) is venting his wrath in great and terrible desperation. But how is he doing this? Through the kingdom of demons which were customarily regarded as the source of man's misery and which Christ had overcome in his ministry, especially in his death on the cross? Not so. There is a special explanation for the present struggle. Other agents are at work on Satan's behalf. These are the two beasts to whom we have already been introduced, the imperial power of the Roman state and the official state priests who conducted emperor worship.

In connection with the dating of the Apocalypse we have previously taken note of emperor worship as it was practiced at the time of its writing. Some passages involving the Nero redivivus myth and the number of the beast (666 or 616) have also been considered.[2] There is yet another statement that John gives as he seeks to identify the agents behind the present catastrophe. It also presents the beast, and it reads as follows:

> And I saw a beast rising out of the sea, with ten horns and seven heads, with ten diadems upon its horns and a blasphemous name upon its heads. And the beast that I saw was like a leopard, its feet were like a bear's, and its mouth was like a lion's mouth. And to it the dragon gave his power and his throne and great authority. One of its heads seemed to have a mortal wound, but its mortal wound was healed, and the whole earth followed the beast with wonder.
>
> —Rev. 13:1-3

The above passage is filled with interest as it speaks of the "sea" from which the sea monster (a leviathan) came, "horns" symbolical of power, "heads" indicating individual persons, and "crowns" suggesting imperial rule.

The numbers seven and ten as found here are best interpreted as referring to rulers who have been in the service of the dragon. Perhaps the figure *ten* is intended to include all the kings that have reigned since Jesus' ministry and *seven*, the leading ones of

[2] Cf. pp. 57-60.

100

this group. When interpreted in this fashion the result would be as follows:

(1)	Tiberius	14-37	(1)
(2)	Caligula	37-41	(2)
(3)	Claudius	41-54	(3)
(4)	Nero	54-68	(4)
(5)	Galba	68-69	
(6)	Otho	69	
(7)	Vitellius	69	
(8)	Vespasian	69-79	(5)
(9)	Titus	79-81	(6)
(10)	Domitian	81-96	(7)

An examination of this chart will show that in the right-hand column the number seven was reached by omitting the names of Galba, Otho, and Vitellius. These were three so-called pretenders to the throne whose periods of rule were too brief to be taken seriously. They were hardly worthy of receiving the dubious honor of being classed with the line of archenemies of Christ who served the dragon and accepted blasphemous divine honors.[3] It should also be noted that the listing ends with Domitian as the last in the sequence. This ties in with the Domitian date for the Apocalypse that we have already considered to be likely. He is not only the present ruling monarch, but he also incorporates all the ignominious sins of those who preceded him.

As in the case of the Four Horsemen of the Apocalypse, there is a prototype for John's beast from the sea in the Old Testament portrayal of the beasts in Daniel 7. There the prophet saw four great beasts, three of which were described thus: the first was like a lion, the second like a bear, and the third like a leopard. These three are combined into a single beast in the Revelation that was like a leopard, with feet like a bear, and a mouth like a lion. Since

[3] Consult the commentaries for other possible reconstructions of the lists of emperors. Some begin with Julius Caesar, count the three pretenders as one rule, and also end with Domitian. All such analyses, including the one we have suggested above, are speculative. Yet they are not without merit if sound historical elements are taken into account.

the three beasts in Daniel represent the world empires of Babylonia (leopard), Media (bear), and Persia (lion), John intends to say that the beast he saw incorporates all the evils of the great pagan powers of the past.

The description of the beast in Revelation 13 also includes a feature that points to the Nero redivivus myth. One of its heads had a mortal wound that had been healed (13:3). The chapter further describes emperor worship and the activities of the Roman priesthood who presided over its practice.

All of this may seem quite tedious to twentieth-century readers. Why did not John come out into the open and state what he meant without recourse to such involved symbolism and cryptic references? We may speak this way because apocalyptic outlook and literary forms are not a part of our environment. They did, however, belong to the first-century world view of Jews and Christians and created much interest and excitement as they dealt in veiled phrases with the mysteries that were to be revealed. They helped the writer to be secretive when he needed to be, lest punishment and premature death should descend upon him and his group. This was not a game of anagrams; it was the spelling out of human destiny.

It has been noted in this chapter that John was not unmoved by the questions that the persecutions and the prospective judgments were raising in the minds of his readers. He sought to answer these in a series of interludes based upon his visions and other traditional apocalyptic writings, both canonical and noncanonical. There was a divine purpose behind the course of events they were facing; it was not a matter of chance or coincidence.

CHAPTER EIGHT

Visions of Hope and Encouragement

We have been considering several interludes whose purpose was to interpret and explain the sufferings that were coming upon the church. In these John sought to answer questions related to the status of those already martyred, the seer's personal involvement, the origin of the struggle on earth, and the agencies that Satan was employing in pursuing his evil course. The answers given pushed the issue back to ultimate causes. Superficial explanations would not do; only those involving the divine ordering of life, historical and suprahistorical, would suffice.

The church in Domitian's day needed not only answers to its questions and explanations of its experiences, but also hope and encouragement. John, who knew personally how painful life could be under these circumstances, was moved to share with his Christian brothers in the great tribulation certain visions that had been granted him. These would strengthen their hearts and brighten their outlook as they gazed into the future through tear-filled eyes.

THE PROTECTION OF THE CHURCH
7:1-8

A real concern of the followers of Christ at this time—and as they looked to the future—was whether or not they would be swallowed up in the judgments that John was announcing. Such all-encompassing destruction must surely bring extinction. What of the faithful in the church? Chapter seven contains an interlude to answer this question, one that is intended to bring assurance and hope to this very group. Imagine their joy when John shared with them his vision of the protective sealing of the servants of God:

> After this I saw four angels standing at the four corners of the earth, holding back the four winds of the earth, that no wind might blow on earth or sea or against any tree. Then I saw another angel ascend from the rising of the sun, with the seal of the living God, and he called with a loud voice to the four angels who had been given power to harm earth and sea, saying, "Do not harm the earth or the sea or the trees, till we have sealed the servants of our God upon their foreheads."
>
> —*Rev. 7:1-3*

What is meant by the sealing? Certainly in this case nothing literal is intended. Does it not refer to a mystic mark, even perhaps to a divine name (22:4), denoting ownership and carrying special protection and privileges? There are canonical and noncanonical parallels for such sealings. In Ezekiel (9:1-8) an angel places an ink mark upon the foreheads of the righteous so that they will not be killed when the sinful citizens of Jerusalem are destroyed. And the Psalms of Solomon (15:8) tell of the marking of the righteous upon their foreheads to protect them from plagues, such as pestilence, sword, and famine. Just so the Christians—those who are marked—will be kept and guarded in the hour of divine visitation. To be sure, their bodies may be destroyed, but their souls will be preserved. A blessed immortality will be granted to them.

Some may ask, "Who shall be saved?" John's answer is that all those who remain faithful shall know this great salvation. This is the meaning of the verses that follow the reference to the sealing. These list the number of the sealed as 144,000, a figure that suggests completeness or fullness, to be selected equally from each of the twelve tribes (7:4-8). Other suggested conclusions are that the 144,000 refer only to the elect of Israel (Rom. 11:5) or to the Jewish Christians. When these views are taken, the vision of those who have washed their robes in the blood of the Lamb, next to be considered, is said to refer to Gentile Christians. On the basis of the primacy of the numbers, rather than the mention of the tribes, however, the interpretation that those marked refer to all the saved seems more likely.

Although there probably is a Hebrew source for this reference to the twelve tribes, it is used here in regard to the faithful in the Christian church which the New Testament views as the New Israel of God. That these tribes are not to be taken literally is evident from the fact that one tribe, Dan, is omitted and that Joseph and Manasseh overlap since the latter comprises part of the former. Accordingly, R. H. Charles concludes that the 144,000 belong to the spiritual, not to the literal, Israel. All peoples and nations and languages make up this group.

THE VICTORY OF THOSE WHO HAVE WASHED
THEIR ROBES IN THE BLOOD OF THE LAMB

7:9-17

It is a characteristic of John as he puts his book together to announce the final victory of the faithful *before it has occurred*. His purpose is to maintain a high level of hope and encouragement among those who are suffering as he describes the dreadful judgments that are to come upon mankind. Visions in which this glorious outcome is foreseen are frequently referred to as proleptic, in the sense that the victory is anticipated in advance. This is what we have in the picture of the ultimate joy of those who have made their robes white in the blood of the Lamb.

The vision that presents this company follows directly upon the heels of the account of the sealing of the faithful, and John may have placed it in this position as a sequel to this interlude. Beckwith has expressed the relationship between the two by saying:

The sealing in the former vision is the promise; the scene in this vision is the promise *realized* [italics mine] in all its fullness when the 12 times 12,000 of the tribes of Israel, the 144,000 of the complete Church of God . . . are seen in their character as an innumerable multitude redeemed out of every nation and people.[1]

[1] I. T. Beckwith, *op. cit.*, p. 268.

We see in this portrayal a tremendous company who stand before the throne (cf. chapter four) and before the Lamb (cf. chapter five) clothed in white robes. They have palm branches in their hands, symbolical of victory (I Macc. 13:51). Within a Christian setting this aspect of the pageant may have called to the reader's minds the paeans of praise to Jesus raised by the pilgrims en route to Jerusalem for the Passover as they broke palm branches and went out to meet him, crying "Hosanna! Blessed be he who comes in the name of the Lord, even the King of Israel!" (John 12:13). In the Revelation, however, the saints sing "Salvation belongs to our God who sits upon the throne, and to the Lamb" (7:10). Whereupon the angels stood round the throne and round the elders and the four living creatures, worshiping God.

This is not all that the vision contains. There is a further identification given of those who are clothed in the white robes. They are the ones who have come out of the great tribulation, the whole church that remains faithful to the end. Although they are clothed in white robes such as were given to the martyrs under the altar (6:11), in my own mind it is difficult to draw the line here between those who are faithful and die a natural death and those who die violently in martyrdom. Despite the statement that these have washed their robes in the blood of the Lamb, this need not necessarily imply that they were martyrs. The New Testament frequently refers to the blood of Jesus that cleanses sinners without any thought of the martyrdom of the saints. Even though it says that these have died in the midst of the tribulation, it is not necessary that they should have been martyred.[2]

But beyond the question of their identity is the description of the life they shall lead after death. The words of the Apocalypse at this point are far too beautiful to paraphrase. This is what it says:

**Therefore are they before the
throne of God,**

[2] For a thoughtful interpretation that identifies this glorious company specifically with martyrs, cf. Martin Rist in *The Interpreter's Bible, op. cit.*, pp. 420-24.

and serve him day and night
within his temple;
and he who sits upon the throne
will shelter them with his presence.
They shall hunger no more, neither
thirst any more;
the sun shall not strike them, nor
any scorching heat.
For the Lamb in the midst of the
throne will be their shepherd,
and he will guide them to springs
of living water;
and God will wipe away every tear
from their eyes."
—*Rev. 7:15-17*

These phrases speak for themselves with a tenderness that can better be felt than analyzed.

SAVED IN SUFFERING
11:1-13

The temple probably symbolizes the saints, since at the time of its horror and cruelty, is also intended to strengthen the faith of the church at the time that it was involved in the midst of the Domitian persecution and the attendant judgments of God. It opens with a vision in which the seer was given a measuring rod and told to measure the temple of God and the altar and those who worshiped there. The outer court of the Gentiles was not to be included. This measuring, like the sealing of the 144,000 is intended to suggest protection, concern, and care for the faithful. The temple probably symbolizes the saints, since at the time of writing the actual temple in Jerusalem was in ruins.

The need for this protective act was great, as the rest of the vision makes clear. It pictures two witnesses, possibly considered as an incarnation of Elijah and Moses, or perhaps typical of all in the church who were called to bear their testimony in the evil hour. And with what might they testified! Like Elijah, whose prayer brought down fire from heaven (II Kings 1:9-16) and who caused a drought to come upon the land (I Kings 17:1), and like Moses, who was associated with the plagues that beset Egypt —particularly the first where water was turned to blood (Exod. 7:17) and the seventh in which hail fell mingled with fire (Exod. 9:23)—the two witnesses have terrific power. There is strength indeed in the word of these who testify for Christ.

One additional fact about them is noted: the period of their ministry is said to be 1,260 days. During this time the forces of evil will persecute the Christians, even as in Daniel the Syrian ruler Antiochus Epiphanes was expected to persecute the Jews for a certain period prior to the end of the age (Dan. 9:27; 12:7).

In spite of the power of the witnesses, the vision indicates that there would come a time when the beast (Antichrist) would kill them. These faithful ones will be martyred, and their bodies left to lie unburied in the streets of the great and evil city of the present world order—a terrific indignity. It will seem as though evil has triumphed; the non-Christian world will make merry, exchanging gifts in celebration. But this is not to be the final state of things. Even as in Ezekiel the valley of dry bones came to life (37:10, 14), God will act to resurrect the two witnesses and take them victoriously to heaven (11:11-12).[3]

What would all of this mean to John's original readers? Would it not say to them that they were living in the difficult period just prior to the end of time, when the forces of the beast (Antichrist) were beating upon them? And would it not also call upon them to bear their testimony of power with faith and confidence? Even though they would quite likely be killed for their witness and suffer great indignities, God would surely save them in a mighty act of deliverance.

[3] The reader should consult the commentaries for a more detailed interpretation of this significant interlude. There are other fascinating and illuminating analogies that might be drawn.

PURSUED BUT DELIVERED

12:1-6

As we examine these interludes we come to the conclusion that John is somewhat like Jesus who once asked, "What is the kingdom of God like? And to what shall I compare it?" (Luke 13:18). Whereupon he immediately proceeded to give several parables by which to illustrate its nature. In a similar vein, our author attempts again and again through a variety of formulations to say to the Christians of his day that evil times are upon them; and he calls for patience, persistence, and even martyrdom. If they remain true to the end they will be saved. Interlude follows interlude, presenting this theme. The symbolism changes from parenthesis to parenthesis, but the purpose remains the same.

The passage we are immediately considering presents another of these interludes that seek to encourage the faithful, and as in the case of some of the others—if not all—the material itself rests upon earlier sources. The author, as usual, has been inspired to put it to the use immediately at hand, and freely adapts it to announce the message the Lord would have him present at this very time.

In this particular instance, the original upon which the interlude is based appears to be a myth with astral features, of which there were many in the ancient world. Some that offer suggestive possibilities are the Greek myth of the birth of Apollo, the Persian myth of the conflict between the good spirit Ormazd and the evil spirit Ahriman, and the Egyptian myth that tells of Isis, the mother of the gods who must flee from a dragon to a place of seclusion where she rears her child Horus. Even though the source of the interlude may originally have been non-Hebraic, by John's time it probably had been taken over into Jewish folklore.

It is the message of the interlude, however, that concerns us most at this point. What did John want to say to the church in the portrayal of the woman clothed with the sun, with the moon under her feet, and on her head a crown of twelve stars? As she gave birth to her child that was caught up to heaven when threatened by a dragon and fled to a place of safety prepared for her by God in the wilderness for 1,260 days, what was the word of the Lord that was intended? Quite briefly, the woman is the ideal Church, the child is the Messiah (ideally rather than historically represented), and the dragon is Satan. We are not to look here for the Virgin Mary or for the birth of Jesus of Nazareth. Instead we are to grasp the truth that from eternity the victory of the Messiah was assured against all attacks of evil. Thus in heaven the eternal triumph was already a fact. Of course, if it was assured *in heaven,* the implications for those on earth were that it will be assured for them *in history.* Here was strength and courage for the faithful.

12:13-17

The verses that follow the portrayal just discussed (7-12) have already been considered in the previous chapter.[4] They present the picture of Michael's war and Satan's expulsion. In verses 13-17, however, John takes up again the figure of the woman who is pursued by the dragon. This time the reference would seem to be more directly related to the historical situation. Before, she was in heaven; now, she is on earth.

The dragon once again pursues the woman as she goes to the wilderness to be protected for a time, and times, and half a time (an equivalent in the Apocalypse for three-and-a-half years and for 1,260 days). But she escapes, for the earth opens its mouth and swallows up the river which the dragon had poured from his mouth as he sought to engulf her. Then the dragon makes war on the rest of her offspring, "those who keep the commandments of God and bear testimony to Jesus" (12:17).

Here again the woman is the ideal Church or people of God that are delivered and kept in safety during the time of the calamities. Her children on earth must still suffer persecution from Satan, but the security of the ideal Church carries with it the assurance of victory for the saints who suffer in John's day. They will take

[4] Cf. pp. 98-99,

110

confidence from this fact and will be encouraged to hold fast in their testimony.

SONGS OF VICTORY
14:1-5
15:2-4

One of the outstanding elements in the visions of the throne room in heaven (chapters four and five) was the glorious singing that perpetually characterized the celestial environment. We are not surprised to discover that in some of the anticipatory visions found in the interludes there are portrayals of choirs singing magnificent choruses. These may well be typical of some of the hymns of the early church.

It has been said that it is impossible to defeat a singing army. Songs elevate the human spirit, filling it with strength and energy. The other interludes we have been examining have dealt with visions of victory based upon events in heaven and on earth. Some were terrifically sobering, even though they promised the ultimate overthrow of Satan. Their message had to be deduced, considered, thought about; it was not immediately evident. Not so with the songs in the present passages. They spoke immediately to the hearts of those who read John's words—they continue to speak to ours.

The first interlude (14:1-5) depicts the 144,000 who have the Father's name written upon their foreheads (the seal of chapter seven?) standing on Mount Zion with the Lamb. They are being taught the song of the redeemed as they listen to the voices of the angelic choir. It is like the sound of many waters, like the sound of loud thunder, like the sound of harpers playing on their harps. What variety! All the emotions of the heart are here. It is a *new song* that is heard, for it is a new hour of victory, since this is a vision for those who, through Christ, shall soon overcome the dragon. It is being sung as though the event had already occurred.

What is it that the redeemed sing? The present passage does not give us the words. The second interlude (15:2-4), however, does detail the phrases of a song that is appropriately called "the song of

111

Moses, the servant of God, and the song of the Lamb." When the children of Israel were brought successfully across the Red Sea they sang of their deliverance (Exod. 15:1 ff.). Just so, those who are guided safely through the struggle with Satan will sing of him who saved them:

> "Great and wonderful are thy
>   deeds,
> O Lord God the Almighty!
> Just and true are thy ways,
> O King of the ages!
> Who shall not fear and glorify thy
>   name, O Lord?
> For thou alone art holy.
> All nations shall come and worship
>   thee,
> for thy judgments have been re-
>   vealed."
> —*Rev. 15:3b-4*

Perhaps this interlude, more than any of the others, would have brought courage and hope to the suffering Christians. Their struggle had not yet ended, but they had already heard the song of triumph they would one day be singing in the hour of victory. And they most surely took this song into their hearts.

In this chapter we have been considering some of the interludes that John introduces between the visions of judgment as he pictures the events that lead up to the end of time. They brought meaning into the present struggle. Particularly, they stirred up anew the hope of the faithful as they promised ultimate victory to those who hold out in the face of the dragon—even through death and martyrdom to a glorious immortality.

CHAPTER NINE

The Doom of Babylon

The person who puts his feeling as well as his mind into reading the book of Revelation cannot miss the sense of growing intensity in outlook as the writing moves toward its conclusion. The temptation to chart this movement with chronological exactness becomes increasingly acute. That there is a structure and a pattern here is quite evident.

On the other hand, it has always seemed to me that we do violence to the creative freedom of the author if we formalize his writing extensively. It is too much like attempting to systematize the aurora borealis with its pulsating streams of light and color as they are seen to rise and fall in the heavens. To be sure, there is a reason for this electrical phenomenon; it rests on a system of relationships in the physical order. But its glory does not lie here, nor does its message to the aesthetic spirit of man.

The systematizers in the study of the Apocalypse have sometimes become too enamored of the program of events that attend the coming of the end of history. Because of this they have done violence to the poetic quality of the work by forcing it into a mold. Even the message has become deformed by pressuring it into a formalized system.

Never in all literary history—to say nothing of biblical writing —has there been a more versatile author than John of the Apocalypse. His great inspirations, the word of God in his visions, have been phrased with a creative originality that is daring and unique. As an apocalyptist he fits the usual pattern, but as a writer and visionary he is not bound by it. How he has suffered at the hands of legalistic, unimaginative, and unschooled interpreters! This is a warning to us as we turn to the closing scenes in the drama of the Revelation.

Sometimes it is necessary to look back if one is to move forward significantly. Thus far in our study of the Apocalypse to John we have taken note of the fact that it must be read within the context of the biblical view of history. In itself it is a philosophy of human-divine events as these are seen to come to a head in the crises that attend the end of time.

It has also been recognized that the Revelation, both as a thought form and a literary work, belongs to a particular type of experience and writing. This must be understood at the outset if its way of thinking and expression is to be followed intelligently. In addition to this, the work must be rooted and grounded in the life situation from which it came. It has an historical background that can be known and an audience of first readers whose needs and problems may be clearly described. The author was writing to this situation and to these persons rather than to us. In the economy of providence, however, God has seen fit to use this book as a vehicle for expressing his divine word to succeeding generations, even up to and including our own day.

We have noted next that the Apocalypse opens with a series of chapters that set the stage for the unfolding drama. They present the vision of one like unto a son of man who is the authority behind the revelation as well as the agent of its fulfillment. This is followed by a description of conditions on earth where the events to be pictured are to take place, as well as by a glimpse into the status of heaven from which the future is to descend.

The writer then turns to a threefold series of visions (seals, trumpets, bowls) that depict the preliminary judgments that are to come upon evil men and nations. These are preparatory to the Final Assize, when the forces of good and evil, of Christ and the dragon, will be locked in mortal combat. They are partial and incomplete; yet, at the same time they are terribly real.

Interlaced between the threefold series, which is essentially one basic act of judgment that is viewed from three aspects, are a number of visions that break the flow of events. These are mostly found between the trumpets and bowls representations, and have been referred to as interludes. Their purpose is to explain and interpret to the church what is taking place in order that its pressing questions might be answered. In addition to this, they are intended to encourage the faithful as they face persecution and martyrdom by presenting proleptic visions of the ultimate victory of Christ, and the beatific blessedness of all who place their trust in him and are loyal to the end.

This review brings us to the present point in our study of the Revelation. We are now ready to turn to the description of the closing events that attend the final destruction of evil, the judgment of the wicked, and the victory of the saints in Christ.

WHAT A CITY!

17:1-6

A major place in the closing events of the drama of the end of the age is given to the fall of the city of Rome. This is no accident; it is not a diversionary interest of John. Great cities (it is likewise true of small communities) are more than an aggregate of persons. They become a point of view, a tour de force in a certain direction, and an atmosphere of reality that all but achieves a metaphysical existence.

To live in a city is to breathe in its spirit, as well as to take into one's lungs its air. Ideals and ideas commingle with smog and traffic. These, however, are not limited to the residents alone; all who pass through or remain for a visit are likewise touched, and to some extent changed, by its life. In addition, those who do business with merchants in a city, as well as those who relate themselves to its official governmental life, participate in its character.

With these thoughts in mind let us turn to a consideration of the place that the city of Rome, called Babylon, holds in the book of Revelation. Two full chapters and part of a third (16:17—18: 24) present her character and downfall. Probably no other community of antiquity has been so castigated as this so-called eternal city. Her sins are described, her destruction announced, and her demise detailed by John in a doom dirge of great beauty.

Why did the author of the Apocalypse go to such lengths? It almost seems as though he gives a disproportionate attention to this city that rests upon seven hills. That is, it seems this way until it is recalled that Rome was regarded as the center of the empire, the seat of the two beasts who were in the service of the dragon. She is not, therefore, just a city among other cities: she is the earthly source of the evils that challenge the forces of righteousness, and her overthrow is prophetic of the defeat of Satan. Moreover, it is the actual beginning of the final triumph of God in history.

In one of the most dramatic portrayals of the Apocalypse we see the city of Rome symbolized by a great harlot who is seated upon the scarlet beast that was depicted in chapter thirteen. The writer's description here must be read to be appreciated.

> And he carried me away in the Spirit into a wilderness, and I saw a woman sitting on a scarlet beast which was full of blasphemous names, and it had seven heads and ten horns. The woman was arrayed in purple and scarlet, and bedecked with gold and jewels and pearls, holding in her hand a golden cup full of abominations and the impurities of her fornication; and on her forehead was written a name of mystery: "Babylon the great, mother of harlots and of earth's abominations." And I saw the woman, drunk with the blood of the saints and the blood of the martyrs of Jesus.
>
> —*Rev. 17:3-6*

This woman is a harlot because through her relationship to imperial power she has turned men away from their true loyalty to God (cf. Isa. 1:21; Hos. 4:12) and caused them to practice idolatry. As a city she is one with the beast upon which she is seated, even seeming to rise from out his being since his scarlet coloring may be seen upon her own garments. Abomination, fornication, and impurities are the words that are best suited to describe her actions. Not only is her own life sinful, but she has also polluted all who have come into contact with her. Like professional harlots and courtesans in that day, she bears on her forehead a headband or fillet, indicating her character and name. It reads "Babylon the great, mother of harlots and of earth's abominations."

There is one touch more that should not be missed. She who had caused the kings of the earth to commit fornication with her and had made them drunk with this evil wine, was herself drunk— drunk with the blood of the saints and the blood of the martyrs of Jesus. This is the supreme indignity, sin, and degradation.

All indications point to the fact that the name Babylon signifies Rome and not Jerusalem.[1] The harlot is said to be seated on many waters (17:1) as well as upon seven hills (17:9). Let not the fact that she is seated upon these and also upon the beast (17:3) confuse you. The logic of apocalyptic representation does not call for complete consistency in its pictorializations. Each of these statements is true in its own way. Another consideration that argues for Rome in the references to Babylon is that, like this ancient city, she was the capital of a world-wide empire, wealthy, powerful, and sinful. It is also thought-provoking to consider that the name Babylon may have been used in John's day to camouflage the reference to the intended city, lest unfriendly eyes might fall upon the writing and accuse the church of treason.

In a deeper sense, even though the historical setting in John's day and his interpretation of the two beasts calls for an identification of Babylon with Rome, the evils that are lifted up are typical of major cities in all times. In his commentary on the Revelation H. B. Swete notes that Arethas, who was a writer of the tenth century, stated that he would not identify Babylon with Rome; it seemed more appropriate for the city of Constantine.[2] Although this is not sound historical interpretation, it may be pertinent re-

---

[1] For a commentary treatment, however, that interprets Babylon as referring to Jerusalem see M. R. Newbolt, *The Book of Unveiling* (London: S.P.C.K., 1952), pp. 168-73.

[2] H. B. Swete, *The Apocalypse of St. John* (London: Macmillan & Co., Ltd., 1922), p. 211.

ligious interpretation. There is a quality to John's writing that makes even his historical references seem contemporary.

THE FALL OF AN IMPERIAL POWER
17:7-18

In connection with this picture of Rome the author makes another attempt to identify the beast upon which the harlot sat. We have already examined his words in chapter thirteen to this same end. In the present passage he says:

> The beast that you saw was, and is not, and is to ascend from the bottomless pit and go to perdition; and the dwellers on earth whose names have not been written in the book of life from the foundation of the world, will marvel to behold the beast, because it was and is not and is to come. This calls for a mind with wisdom: the seven heads are seven hills on which the woman is seated; they are also seven kings, five of whom have fallen, one is, the other has not yet come, and when he comes he must remain only a little while. As for the beast that was and is not, it is an eighth but it belongs to the seven, and it goes to perdition.
>
> —*Rev. 17:8-11*

Following these words John adds that the ten horns of the beast (cf. 17:12) are ten kings. These are probably the Parthian governors (satraps) from the East who will be recognized as kings for a brief time. They are under the control of the Antichrist and at his direction will make war against the Lamb, only to be conquered. The reader may wish to turn to the chart of Roman emperors on page 159 in an attempt to relate these cryptic words to the first-century rulers. Certainly he will want to consult the commentaries for the numerous attempts at solutions to this puzzle—for puzzle it surely is—that are suggested. If John were deliberately intending to be obscurantist he could hardly have succeeded more soundly, for the answer is far from obvious. Once again, as in chapter thirteen, he does not indicate the ruler with which the figuring should begin. It might actually be questioned as to how completely he was informed concerning the succession of first-century emperors.

The following chart taken from Beckwith is suggestive.[3] It does not answer our question with any finality, but it does indicate certain possible ways of figuring.

Caesar	1	1		
Augustus	2	2	1	1
Tiberius	3	3	2	2
Caligula	4	4	3	3
Claudius	5	5	4	4
Nero	6	6	5	5
Galba	7		6	
Otho	8		7	
Vitellius			8	
Vespasian		7		6
Titus		8		7
Domitian				8

While the last column is more in harmony with the view that Domitian is the final ruler in the line and the incarnation of Nero, it seems to place the author's date in the rule of Vespasian. This does not fit what the Apocalypse implies elsewhere.

Perhaps the solution to this riddle does not lie in close numerical figuring but, rather, in John's thought pattern. His general purpose is to prophesy the fall of the imperial Roman power, to indicate its nearness, and to identify the work of the Antichrist. To

[3] Cf. I. T. Beckwith, op. cit., p. 704.

this end, the seven kings may be said to represent the full content of the cult that practiced emperor worship. Five of them have already died. One of this number that has died is to come again (Nero redivivus) as the Antichrist. The latter is also referred to as an eighth and, as such, succeeds the Roman power represented by the seven kings.

Some solution along these lines supports John's evaluation of the emperor cult as completely evil and fully representing the work of the dragon. At the same time it reaffirms his position concerning the ruling Caesar's relation to the Nero redivivus myth. Finally, it highlights his particular view of the place of the Antichrist in the unfolding drama of human destiny.

THE FALL OF AN IMPERIAL CITY
16:17-21; 18:1-24

With the prophecy of the fall of the imperial Roman power in hand, John turns next to the matter of the fall of the imperial Roman city—the Babylon portrayed so graphically in chapter seventeen. In a kind of proleptic description of this event, he has already shown her demolition.

> **The great city was split into three parts, and the cities of the nations fell, and God remembered great Babylon, to make her drain the cup of the fury of his wrath. And every island fled away, and no mountains were to be found; and great hailstones, heavy as a hundredweight, dropped on men from heaven, till men cursed God for the plague of the hail, so fearful was that plague.**
>
> **—Rev. 16:19-21**

In spite of the vividness of this statement (the seventh bowl), the author is not content to let the matter rest. He moves ahead in chapter eighteen and presents a typical Hebrew dirge, lamenting the fall of the city. Do not be misled; it is not John who weeps for her, but her friends—those who have done business with her.

First of all, the people of God are urged to come out of the city (18:4-8). If they remain they will be in danger both of participating in her sins and of being visited by the plagues that are to come upon her. And how great are these sins! They are heaped, pile upon pile, as high as heaven. So heinous are they that the seer thinks of retribution twice over the usual measure, saying "mix a double draught for her in the cup she mixed" (18:6). But the city does not regard herself; she says "A queen I sit, I am no widow, mourning I shall never see" (18:7). She is tragically mistaken; the blindness to sin that sin itself brings has closed her eyes to her own plight. Her plagues will come upon her "in a single day." That which took centuries to build will be cast down all at once.

John next invites us to gaze upon the doom of Rome through the eyes of those who have been related to her ongoing life. These are they who have done business with her and have participated in her wantonness (18:9-20). First of all there are the kings. Since they were related to her idolatries, they are accused of having committed fornication with her (18:9-10). From afar they will "see the smoke of her burning" and in fear cry "Alas! Alas!" She had been a mighty city—once. Now in one hour she has fallen.

Rome had not only been politically powerful; she had also known a vigorous economic life. This is felt acutely in the lamenting of the merchants whose coffers she had filled (18:11-17a). Like the kings they, too, stand far off (it is no longer safe to be near) and weep at the city's downfall. No one will buy their cargo anymore. And what a cargo it was! John lists the articles of trade as including "gold, silver, jewels and pearls, fine linen, purple, silk and scarlet, all kinds of scented wood, all articles of ivory, all articles of costly wood, bronze, iron and marble, cinnamon, spice, incense, myrrh, frankincense, wine, oil, fine flour and wheat, cattle and sheep, horses and chariots" (18:12-13). Then, with a penetrating and rapierlike thrust, the seer adds to the listing, "and slaves, that is, human souls." This was the great sin. It is possible that our author was not thinking of the institution of slavery as such; instead, he may have had in mind the destruction of persons that resulted from the apostasy Rome encouraged in the enforcing of emperor worship. On the other hand, we may actually have here a deeply humanitarian upsurge, touched off by the moral seriousness of the hour of judgment, in which the sins of the slave traffic were acutely seen in all their tragic consequences. The fact that the souls of men are included in this list of material goods is itself a condemnation of slavery. Persons can never be classed as properties.

There is yet another group in the dirge through whose eyes the fall of Rome is viewed. These are the sailors, shipmasters, and seafaring men (18:17b-20). It is the business of such as these to gaze at the horizon. Beyond are the ports. It is a significant moment when the creaking hulk settles down in its berth, and every hour at sea looks toward that goal. No more—as far as Rome is concerned. Instead of the familiar signs on the shore, there was smoke rising into the heavens, and the sailors "cried out as they saw the smoke of her burning."

When the end arrives (18:21-24) there is desolation, darkness, and silence:

> "So shall Babylon the great city be
>   thrown down with violence,
>   and shall be found no more;
> and the sound of harpers and minstrels, of flute players and
>   trumpeters,
>   shall be heard in thee no more;
> and a craftsman of any craft
>   shall be found in thee no more;
> and the sound of the millstone
>   shall be heard in thee no more;
> and the light of a lamp
>   shall shine in thee no more;
> and the voice of bridegroom and
>   bride
>   shall be heard in thee no more;
> for thy merchants were the great
>   men of the earth,

and all nations were deceived by
thy sorcery.
And in her was found the blood of
prophets and of saints,
and of all who have been slain on
earth."
—*Rev. 18:21b-24*

Music, the sound of laborers, light, the joyful voices of brides and bridegrooms—all are forever stilled. Such pathos and beauty of expression have rarely been joined together in world literature.

Similarities between this chapter and the dirge over the fall of Tyre in Ezekiel (27-28) are most suggestive.[4] That John was familiar with it can hardly be doubted. It should not be concluded, however, that he has given us a pale copy of this earlier prototype. His creative originality is evident as the words of the dirge are read in the light of the actual situation in Rome at the time of the author's writing.

In this chapter we have taken a long look at the doom of Babylon, interpreted as the city of Rome. Her place in the campaign of Satan against Christ has been so pivotal that her destruction, as a prelude to the final judgment, deserves particular attention. John is now ready to move ahead in his account of the end of human history.

---

[4] For other interesting examples of dirge songs cf. Isa. 13:19-22; 34:5 ff.; Jer. 50:35 ff.; Zeph. 2:12 ff.

CHAPTER TEN

The Final Judgment

The destruction of the city of Rome that was the theme of the previous chapter is not simply the demolition of a city. As we have already noted, it is a prelude to the final combat. Here is to be the resolving of the issue between Christ and his forces (the martyrs and the angels) and the hosts of Satan, the dragon (his beasts and those who follow them). This is known as the battle of Armageddon.

ARMAGEDDON

19:11-21

With the emptying of the sixth bowl of the wrath of God three frog spirits, unclean and despicable, were sent forth by the dragon to summon "the kings of the whole world . . . for battle on the great day of God the Almighty" (16:14). Daniel (11:45) and Ezekiel (39:1 ff.) locate such a conflict in the midst of the mountains of Israel. Mount Megiddo, which should be translated "hill of victory" is the original meaning of the word "Armageddon" in Hebrew. It is interesting by way of background to recall that the battle of Deborah took place on the plains of Megiddo (Judges 5:19). It seems to me, however, that we are dealing here predominately with ideas and issues rather than with site and geography.

The battle of Armageddon is so significant that John leads his readers to the event gradually. This is a part of his technic for creating interest; it also represents his desire to linger a bit on the edge of the precipice as he prepares them for the last scene. Before presenting this final struggle, he gives us a song of triumph in heaven. The celestial choir sings of the judgment of the great harlot (19:1-3); the twenty-four elders cry "Amen. Hallelujah" (19:4); even from the throne one hears a voice praising God, he who is about to act in the denouement of history (19:5). And then the coming marriage of Christ, the Lamb, with his Bride, the Church, is announced (19:6-8). Her wedding gown is described as being woven of none other than the "righteous deeds of the saints." What glorious imagery this! All who are invited to the marriage supper are said to be blessed (19:9).

Still more is needed before the portrayal of Armageddon itself. John has taken pains to describe one of the opponents, the beast. The other, Christ, has not been pictured with any detail since the opening chapters of the Apocalypse. Surely we cannot be asked to view the battle without once again gazing upon him who is to defend the saints, execute God's judgment, and conquer the dragon and his cohorts. We must look with awe and breathless expectation at the warrior-Messiah:

> Then I saw heaven opened, and behold, a white horse! He who sat upon it is called Faithful and True, and in righteousness he judges and makes war. His eyes are like a flame of fire, and on his head are many diadems; and he has a name inscribed which no one knows but himself. He is clad in a robe dipped in blood, and the name by which he is called is The Word of God. And the armies of heaven, arrayed in fine linen, white and pure, followed him on white horses. From his mouth issues a sharp sword with which to smite the nations, and he will rule them with a rod of iron; he will tread the wine press of the fury of the wrath of God the Almighty. On his robe and on his thigh he has a name inscribed, King of kings and Lord of lords.
>
> —Rev. 19:11-16

Christ is seen here in his supreme power over evil forces, such forces as were actually threatening the first readers. As the conquering warrior-Messiah from heaven, he rides a white horse followed by an army of celestial martyrs clad in linen, pure and white. With eyes like a flame of fire, his head crowned with many crowns, and his robe dipped in the blood of his enemies, he is an awesome figure. Out of his mouth extends a sharp sword with which to smite the nations (cf. 1:16).

In addition Christ, the warrior-Messiah, is represented in this vision as possessing several names; three are known, and one is a secret. All the significance attributed to names in Hebrew apocalyptic is brought to bear upon his designation. He is called Faithful and True, the Word of God, King of kings and Lord of lords. Whatever their derivation, they signify his character as the Messiah. He is true to his mission, imbued with the power of judgment, and supreme over all earthly rulers. The secret name known only to himself adds a further element of power to Christ's person. It was believed at the time that a secret held miraculous potentialities, especially an unknown name (cf. 2:17; 3:12). And the warrior-Messiah has a secret name!

Not only does Christ as this warrior-Messiah have a specific kind of character and significant names—both known and unknown; he also has a mission to fulfill. Even as the messianic figure of Isaiah (11:3-5), he judges in righteousness, a judgment which in this instance is expressed by making war on the Beast. With the sword which issues from his mouth he will overpower and conquer the enemy nations, ruling them with a rod of iron (cf. Ps. 2:9; also Rev. 12:5). In doing this he will be treading, so to speak, "the wine press of the fury of the wrath of God the Almighty" (cf. 14:19-20; Isa. 63:1-6).

Now we are ready to view Armageddon, prepared to witness an extended conflict. But it does not develop. With the opposing forces, earthly and heavenly, arrayed against each other John simply says, "And the beast was captured, and with it the false prophet [the official Roman priesthood][5] who in its presence had worked the signs by which he deceived those who had received the mark of the beast and those who worshiped its image" (19:20).

[5] Brackets mine.

126

Is the reader let down, disappointed, deflated by the brevity of the description of the final issue? Has John exhausted his capacity for brilliant and colorful verbal elaboration? Not so! There is real drama in this paucity of description. No one can hold out before the august warrior-Messiah in the final hour. A prolonged battle would be a contradiction.

THE MILLENNIUM
20:1-6

At the close of the battle of Armageddon the beast and his cohort, the false prophet, were thrown alive into the lake of fire. This was the final seat of punishment for the wicked; it was not the sheol of the Old Testament but the destination of the damned. But what of Satan, "that ancient serpent, who is the Devil"? His ultimate disposition must wait. This does not mean, however, that he is free at this point—not at all! He is bound and cast into a pit that is sealed over to prevent his escape. This is not his final fate, for he will lead one more mad maneuver; but there is to be a temporary respite from his onslaughts.

There is real drama at this point. John foresees the setting up of a special period of beatific blessedness, during which time the work of the dragon is absolutely at a standstill. This is to be the reign of Christ on earth for a thousand years. His subjects, who also share in the reigning, are the martyrs that have died in the struggle:

> Then I saw thrones, and seated on them were those to whom judgment was committed. Also I saw the souls of those who had been beheaded for their testimony to Jesus and for the word of God, and who had not worshiped the beast or its image and had not received its mark on their foreheads or their hands. They came to life again, and reigned with Christ a thousand years. The rest of the dead did not come to life again until the thousand years were ended. This is the first resurrection. Blessed and holy is he who shares in the first resurrection! Over such the second death has no power, but

> they shall be priests of God and of Christ, and they shall
> reign with him a thousand years.
>
> —*Rev. 20:4-6*

There is a divine appropriateness in the coming of the millennium. Christ had never actually known an earthly reign. He had been refused by the Jews as their national leader. A cross, rather than a crown, had been his lot. Even what we call the triumphal entry was short-lived. To be sure, there had been for him a spiritual rule in the church as he became its living Lord, present through the Spirit, and directing its life. In terms of the prophetic expectation of an earthly kingdom for the Messiah, however, there was still some unfinished business. Now it would be completed.

The fact that the martyrs are to reign with him at the same time that they are to be his subjects is also significant. Throughout the Apocalypse the martyrs have been given unusual and tender consideration. You will recall that at their death a special place had been prepared to receive them under the very altar of heaven (6:9 ff.). There they were kept in blessed security until their number had been completed. Now was the hour of fulfillment as they "came to life again, and reigned with Christ a thousand years."

In approaching a study of the millennium we should not miss its religious and spiritual significance. It is not sufficient merely to point out its antecedents in Hebrew, Egyptian, and Persian thought, important as these are. I do not believe that John is placing a millennial reign of Christ in his schematic portrayal of the future just because there had been those before him who had written of a time of special rule. On the other hand, it is significant to note that this idea seemed to have had wide acceptance in the religions of the ancient world. For example, in the eschatology of Zoroastrianism, world history is divided into twelve millenniums, the last of which would be the millennium of the third Saoshyant, who was a sort of messiah.

Among the Hebrews there had long been the hope of the coming of God's kingdom on earth. The dreams of a messianic age and the day of the Lord had prepared the people to expect a special time of God's visitation when the nation's enemies would be put down and her national glory extended. We see this outlook particularly in the writings of the prophets. Later authors, especially the apocalyptists, envisioned this hope in more transcendental terms. They saw in the future a temporary rule on earth of the Messiah together with the righteous. Even some who had already died were included. These ideas were expressed in various forms (II Esdras 12:34; I Enoch 91:12; Apocalypse of Baruch 40:3). They laid the background for John's portrayal of the millennium, perhaps even suggesting it to him. But he was personally inspired as to its truth and transformed it into a Christian theme with Christ and the martyrs at its center. As a Christian reality it was the answer to the petition in the Lord's Prayer: "Thy will be done, on earth as it is in heaven."

When John uses the figure of a thousand years he is speaking symbolically rather than mathematically. The number suggests a limited but sufficient block of time as compared with eternity. It has frequently been pointed out that considerable restraint must have been exercised on the author's part as he describes this period. He does not indulge in the typical descriptions of lush living, sometimes quite sensuous, that others before—and since—have used in picturing millennial reigns. The reason is that the idea is essentially moral and spiritual. Why, then, does he not present an elaborate mosaic of symbols that would carry a spiritual meaning and portray more detail? Is this necessary? Christ is there! The martyrs are there! This is glory enough; it is always poor religion and artistry to gild the lily. Besides, there will be ample opportunity to employ symbols of glory in the portrayal of the new heaven and earth that John will soon present.

In the history of apocalyptic thinking since John's day, even to the present hour, the millennium has been given a prominent position. Different schools of thought have emerged. We have the premillenialists who teach that Christ will return before the thousand years' reign. Then there are the postmillennialists who insist that the kingdom will spread effectively throughout all the world, and then Christ will return. Although the book of Revelation itself is premillenial, this argument as such does not enter the author's mind. I personally think that he would have been impatient with it. In spite of the fact that his writing contains a kind of "schedule of coming events," he is not a legalist or a systematizer to the extent that many of his readers have become.

Following the millennium, events move swiftly to a close. There is a brief resurgence of Satan as he is released from the pit (prison) and leads the nations at the four corners of the earth in a massive and dramatic march against Jerusalem, the seat of the millennial reign of Christ. He is unsuccessful; actually, he never has a chance. Fire comes down from heaven and consumes both him and his followers. Then he is thrown into the lake of fire and brimstone where the beast and the false prophet have already been consigned (19:20). This is the end of Satan. Torment, day and night forever, is all that lies ahead for him and the two beasts, even as it will for those who have followed him and bear his mark (20:15).

As he depicts this last campaign against Christ and his own, John, in referring to Satan and the evil nations, makes use of the traditional expression "Gog and Magog."

> And when the thousand years are ended, Satan will be loosed from his prison and will come out to deceive the nations which are at the four corners of the earth, that is, Gog and Magog, to gather them for battle; their number is like the sand of the sea.
>
> —*Rev. 20:7-8*

He probably introduces Gog and Magog because the words already had become a symbol of an evil attack and a divine deliverance. Ezekiel (38-39) had long since written of an anticipated march of Gog, who lived in the land of Magog, into the mountains of Israel. There he would seek to plunder and destroy. But God

130

would intervene, killing the attackers with hail, fire, and brimstone. Birds and beasts would be assembled from all sides to "eat the flesh of the mighty, and drink the blood of the princes of the earth" (39:18). Thus the enemy will be destroyed. All this seemed highly appropriate in spirit and vernacular to our author as he described the last attack upon the holy city.

The meticulous reader will, no doubt, ask some questions concerning this ill-fated march on Jerusalem—and well he may. The description of Armageddon suggested complete destruction of the earthly forces of evil when it said that "the rest [the kings of the earth of 19:19] were slain by the sword of him who sits upon the horse, the sword that issues from his mouth; and all the birds were gorged with their flesh" (19:21). From whence, then, came the nations at the four corners of the earth who joined forces with Satan after his release from the pit? Only John could have known the answer to this question. Men have guessed and the replies vary. On the other hand, perhaps John himself did not know and did not even care. From his point of view such an inquiry would be purely academic; he was mainly concerned to tell of Satan's impotence before the camp of the saints and of his final overthrow and permanent punishment.

There is the possibility that the march of Gog and Magog against Jerusalem is but a rephrasing of the battle of Armageddon. It was necessary in order to finally dispose of Satan, since his incarceration in the pit was only temporary. One is tempted to inquire why Armageddon did not finally overthrow Satan as it had permanently destroyed the two beasts (19:20). One answer might be that this would have reduced the drama of the millennial reign of the saints with Christ. This was so important that God interrupted the climax of history as it was trembling on the immediate horizon to recognize the Messiah and his loyal followers. Certainly he must have been eager to bring about the dragon's downfall as quickly as possible, but this special glorification of the martyrs with the Lamb took precedence. Satan's ultimate judgment must wait; but when it came it would be truly final.

THE LAST JUDGMENT
20:11-15

The end was at hand; but one event remained. Although it is treated briefly (all the major events in the Apocalypse are so dealt with), it had eternal consequences for the entire human race. Before a great white throne (cf. Revelation 4:2?) the dead, now raised to life from Death, Hades, and the sea, were judged on the basis of the record of their deeds that had been kept in books:

> **Then I saw a great white throne and him who sat upon it; from his presence earth and sky fled away, and no place was found for them. And I saw the dead, great and small, standing before the throne, and books were opened. Also another book was opened, which is the book of life. And the dead were judged by what was written in the books, by what they had done. And the sea gave up the dead in it, Death and Hades gave up the dead in them, and all were judged by what they had done. Then Death and Hades were thrown into the lake of fire. This is the second death, the lake of fire; and if any one's name was not found written in the book of life, he was thrown into the lake of fire.**
>
> **—Rev. 20:11-15**

There was system and order to the solemn procedure. Judgment, John says, was in line with "what they had done." No guesswork this. It was all a matter of record. Although it is not so stated, it must be assumed that the grace of God had already gone into the writing of the books. Even so, there were still those whose names were not written in *the book of life,* that "other book" that contained the list of the faithful—perhaps the 144,000 of chapter seven. These were cast into the lake of fire where Satan and the two beasts had been thrown.

There is a reference in the account of these eventful matters that might easily be overlooked. It simply reads, "Then Death and Hades were thrown into the lake of fire" (20:14). These had long been the enemies of man. Fear, sorrow, and suffering had followed in their train. Now they were to be no more. These sources of evil had finally been destroyed along with Satan and the beasts.

The lake of fire in the Apocalypse is called "the second death" (20:6, 14; 21:8). This is the final judgment in contrast to the first death, which is the cessation of physical life. John also speaks of "the first resurrection" (20:5) at which time the martyrs are revived for the blessed millennium. The second resurrection presumably would be that which was related to the final judgment when all the dead, both good and evil, were raised to stand before the great white throne.

So awesome was the prospect of this final judgment that John notes the flight of earth and heaven (sky) from the presence of God. They could not face the tragedy of this hour. Perhaps, more importantly, earth was too evil to remain; the events that had occurred on her bosom had polluted her beyond renewal. The way is now prepared for the coming of the new heaven and the new earth that the author describes in the last of his visions.

The second epistle of Peter was probably written four or five decades after the Revelation to John. It also refers to the destruction of the heavens with the coming of a new heaven and a new earth:

> But the day of the Lord will come like a thief, and then the heavens will pass away with a loud noise, and the elements will be dissolved with fire, and the earth and the works that are upon it will be burned up. Since all these things are thus to be dissolved, what sort of persons ought you to be in lives of holiness and godliness, waiting for and hastening the coming of the day of God, because of which the heavens will be kindled and dissolved, and the elements will melt with fire! But according to his promise we wait for new heavens and a new earth in which righteousness dwells.
>
> —II Pet. 3:10-13

The similarity between these words and the brief reference to a similar happening in the Revelation cannot be missed. Two differences, however, should be noted. In Second Peter the destruction of the elements is said to be by fire. In addition, the author uses this cataclysmic prospect as an occasion for solemn warning and evangelistic invitation.

In this chapter we have been considering the awesome and sobering events that will bring history to a close and resolve the age-long struggle between good and evil. It is in the face of such a portrayal that the word *destiny* finds its meaning. The true dimensions of our deeds and acts from day to day are only seen as they are viewed in the light of Armageddon, the millennium, and the final judgment. No one who understands what is written about these matters in the Revelation to John can ever again take life lightly. Personal responsibility for one's behavior and dedication to the will of God in the service of Christ are the only answer.

CHAPTER ELEVEN

The Final Glory

The last scene in the book of Revelation is not one of carnage and destruction; rather, it is filled with beauty and beatific blessedness. Up to this point we have seen so much of suffering and judgment that one might decide that the seer took a morbid delight in depicting the somber side of life. But in view of the elaborate description of the final glory that he presents, such a conclusion would be incorrect. John is not a pessimist; he is realistically optimistic.

The fact is that the seer is a true apocalyptist who feels deeply and is personally touched by what he sees in the offing. When judgment lies before him, he paints the scene with unrelieved darkness. But when blessedness brightens the future, the prospect is portrayed with a brilliance that is blinding. The reason for this is not due to his emotional capacities and literary talent. He is basically a philosopher with a specific world view. To him situations must grow worse before they can become better. Human impotence precedes divine deliverance. Both are terribly real and, therefore, each must be seen for what it is; to hold back would be folly.

As we noted in the very beginning of our study, this is the psychology and philosophy of apocalypticism. As opposed to other views of history, those who think, feel, and write within this tradition are committed to the conclusion that the judgment of God rests upon the acts of men and nations. They have become so evil —except for the faithful—that destruction is inevitable. But this is not the end; God will not abdicate his purposes. If they cannot be realized "in time," they will be completed "beyond time."

In the book of Revelation this view is eminently illustrated. We have seen the judgment both predicted and executed, and now we are ready to be shown the deliverance from on high. John has taken twenty chapters to depict the former; he takes but one and part of another to portray the latter. But what writing this is! Symbols, metaphors, word pictures, and dramatic phrases fairly spill over one another in the onrush of emotions and ideas as the beatification of the blessed in Christ is described. Seldom does one find such a density of illustration as is to be met here.

A NEW HEAVEN AND A NEW EARTH

21:1-8

At the close of the preceding chapter the situation that John portrayed made ready for a new development. The forces of evil had been cast into the lake of fire; the dragon, his two beasts, and all that bore his mark—and consequently, did not have their names written in the book of life—had been removed from the earthly scene. Sky, earth, Death, and Hades had been done away with. But what of the saints and martyrs? Where were they to dwell?

The answer to these questions is immediately given with the opening of chapter twenty-one: "Then I saw a new heaven and a new earth; for the first heaven and the first earth had passed away, and the sea [a source of misery and fear] was no more." In addition there was also a new city, the "new Jerusalem, coming down out of heaven from God." Here it was that the faithful shall live. But they shall not be alone; God himself will be with them. Tears, death, mourning, and pain shall be at an end. These belonged to the "former things" that have passed away.

We have already discovered in this study that many of the ideas that the seer presents are not original with him. They have a history as prophets of the past have expressed them. The eternal Spirit of God has been moving through the centuries, and certain major conceptions that have been called forth in the minds of these men of the past John finds pertinent to the situation at hand. When this happens, he does not hesitate to use them, adapting them to the immediate needs of the church. Such is the case with the picture of the new heaven and the new earth.

In the face of the tragedy, sin, and suffering of earth, it was inevitable that men who believed in the goodness of God should dream of a new beginning of some kind. Not only did they think of this for themselves as persons, but they also conceived of it as a renewal of the heavens and the earth. Therefore Isaiah could represent Jehovah as saying, "For behold, I create new heavens and a new earth; and the former things shall not be remembered or come into mind" (65:17). He then moves on to speak of the cessation of weeping and the beauty of the joy that shall come. A similar teaching is found in First Enoch where we read, "I will transform the heaven, and make it an eternal blessing and light. And I will transform the earth and make it a blessing" (45:4 ff.).

Sometimes, however, it has seemed that the desolation has been too great for a renewal to be effected. The old order needs, instead, to be completely replaced. First Enoch, again, speaks in this vein: "The first heaven will depart and pass away, and a new heaven will appear, and all the powers of the heavens will shine sevenfold for ever" (91:16). A great faith in God has lighted the fires of hope; a glowing future lies ahead. It is just this kind of conviction that is at the heart of John's vision of a new heaven and a new earth in the Apocalypse.

The seer finds his hope confirmed when he hears the voice of God saying, "Behold, I make all things new" (21:5). It is from the throne, the seat of the eternal rule of the Divine, that God speaks. The authority behind the promise is therefore assured. H. B. Swete has called to our attention that this is probably the first time that God himself has been the speaker in the Revelation.[1] Christ and the angels have been heard again and again. But now it is God the creator who is announcing the *new creation*. He does more than this; he commands John to write down the words because they are "trustworthy and true." How long ago it must have

---

[1] H. B. Swete, *The Apocalypse of St. John* (London: Macmillan & Co., Ltd., 1922), p. 279. This conclusion must relate only to the series of visions themselves, since in 1:8 God is most likely the speaker.

seemed to the seer that Christ had given him a similar injunction! It was at the very beginning of his prophetic experience that he heard behind him as he was in the Spirit on the Lord's day a voice, loud like a trumpet, saying, "Write what you see in a book and send it to the seven churches" (1:11). How loyally he has obeyed this command! We who have been following the Revelation can well bear witness to this fact.

There is yet another announcement that is made at this time. It is the hour for great affirmations. In the light of what has happened—the destruction of Satan and his followers, the judgment of sinners, the dissolution of earth, sea, and sky, the descent of a new heaven and a new earth—it is appropriate that utterances of terrific finality should be made. When, therefore, God says, "It is done! I am the Alpha and the Omega, the beginning and the end" (21:6), who would question that this is true? Has it not already been shown to be a fact? The reader will recognize that Alpha and Omega are the first and last letters in the Greek alphabet. Jewish rabbis sometimes expressed the eternity of God in a similar fashion, using the first and last letters of the Hebrew alphabet. We would do well to recall also that in the very beginning of the Apocalypse an identical announcement was made (1:8). He who is the beginning and the end has spoken at the beginning and at the end. The eternal God eternally speaks, even as he is the creator and the omnipotent ruler.

THE BRIDE, THE WIFE OF THE LAMB

21:9

We have previously noted that the new heaven and the new earth must have a new city—and it has. This is the holy city Jerusalem which comes down out of heaven where it has been all along as an ideal counterpart of the earthly Jerusalem that is no more. Even as Ezekiel had seen a vision of a restored Israel with a new temple (Ezek. 40-48), so John is given a vision of the new Jerusalem which, as we shall see, was both city and temple.

It is significant to note that it was one of the seven angels who carried the seer away in the Spirit to view this celestial sight (21:9-

10). It had also been one of the seven angels who had borne John away, likewise in the Spirit, to see Babylon, the great harlot (17:1-3). In both cases he had said, "Come, I will show you." But how dissimilar the view! The comparison should not be missed. This is high drama; it is also high religion. Men may take their choice—Babylon the harlot or the new Jerusalem, the Bride. John wants his readers to see that in their very own day they were actually making this same selection—and men have been making it ever since.

This reference to the new Jerusalem as the Bride, the wife of the Lamb, calls to mind the previous announcement or beatitude: "Blessed are those who are invited to the marriage supper of the Lamb" (19:9). Her wedding garments had already been described as pure white linen, woven out of the "righteous deeds of the saints" (19:8). Beauty and purity were here joined together. This is not the first time that the symbol of marriage has been used in the scriptures to define a relationship with God. Jehovah had long ago said to Israel, "I will betroth you to me for ever; I will betroth you to me in righteousness and in justice, in steadfast love, and in mercy. I will betroth you to me in faithfulness; and you shall know the Lord." (Hos. 2:19-20.) More recently, the apostle Paul had written to the church at Corinth, saying "I feel a divine jealousy for you, for I betrothed you to Christ to present you as a pure bride to her one husband" (II Cor. 11:2).

In the Hosea passage it was Israel that was the bride; in the Pauline letter it was the church as the New Israel. When the seer sees the holy city Jerusalem as the bride, he is thinking within the same context, for Jerusalem and the people of Israel are often identified as one (cf. Gal. 4:25, Isa. 40:1 ff.). We have here a tremendously significant conception. Christ and the Church are presented as belonging together in terms of the most spiritual and intimate of all personal relationships.

THE NEW JERUSALEM

21:9-27

The description of the city is highly symbolical, extravagantly so. It is as E. F. Scott has written in referring to John's method of composition here, when he notes that the writer has

heaped up all the images of beauty and delight that he can think of. Some of them he derives from the early chapters of Genesis; some from the Psalms and Prophets; some from apocalyptic; some from his acquaintance with famous cities of his own time. All has been heightened by his imagination and bathed in the light of religious ideas. Although the picture cannot be made consistent, it conveys in marvellous fashion the conception of a place altogether glorious, which will be the fitting abode of the people of God.[2]

From one standpoint, to separate, for purposes of analysis, the various elements that comprise the picture is like severing the parts of a blossom from the cup holding them together in order to examine them more closely. When you have finished, you no longer have a flower—although you may have increased your knowledge. Beauty has given way to botanical information. Yet, there is true beauty in an understanding of composition for those who look beneath the surface of life. It is thus with a study of such biblical passages as the portrayal of the new Jerusalem. The message becomes clearer when the several facets that make up the scene are considered separately.

STRUCTURE AND DIMENSIONS

In the first place, the structure and dimensions of the city are most unusual. When measured with "a measuring rod of gold" it turns out to be foursquare. The giant cube is about 1,500 miles on each side and, as someone has noted, this would take in more area than is contained in all of Palestine. What is the point of this feature of the city? Does it not say to the reader that there is perfect symmetry (how esthetically satisfying) and adequacy (there would be room for all) to the place God has prepared for his own?

[2] E. F. Scott, *The Book of Revelation* (New York: Charles Scribner's Sons, 1940), pp. 99-100.

The holy of holies in the temple was also cubical (I Kings 6:20).

A city of such height would reach far into the sky so that earth and heaven would seem to unite. Was not John thinking of what the writer in the Sibylline Oracles (V, p. 251 ff., 424 ff.) had in mind when he conceived of the walls of Jerusalem in the final days as reaching "up to the darkling clouds," and its tower "touching the very clouds and seen of all, so that all the faithful and all the righteous may see the glory of the invisible God"? Religious ideas rather than architecture are central in this representation. One wonders what is in the minds of Christians today who sing of the city foursquare, especially at funeral services. If they are literal-minded they will miss the true glory of the seer's vision.

All about this city is a wall containing twelve gates. Perhaps, if the author had been writing now, this feature would have been missing from the picture. We do not place walls about our towns, nor do we have gates for entrance to our communities, but these were basic in the ancient world. The walls protected the cities from enemy attack and the gates controlled both entry and exit. Because of this the life story of major cities could almost be told in terms of its walls and gates.

Judging by actual figures a wall about 216 feet tall—which was the height of the one that surrounded the city—would be much higher than usual and more than adequate for its intended purpose. This, no doubt, was what John wanted to indicate about the wall. Its height measured in terms of cubits was 144, which is the square of twelve (in Ezek. 40:5; 42:20, it is the thickness of the wall that is stressed). This also implies perfection or completeness. But what a contrast there is between the 216 foot wall and the 1,500 mile city! What has happened to the author's sense of proportion? Perhaps nothing has occurred. Each contributes its own idea in its own way. And yet the relationship remains intriguing. One interesting suggestion that has been made is that the incongruity between the height of the wall and the area of the city is intended to accentuate the tremendous size of the latter. It is the city itself that is central.

141

GATES AND FOUNDATION

Reference has already been made to the fact that the walls had twelve gates. John describes them by saying, "It had a great, high wall, with twelve gates, and at the gates twelve angels, and on the gates the names of the twelve tribes of the sons of Israel were inscribed; on the east three gates, on the north three gates, on the south three gates, and on the west three gates" (21:12-13). Upon reading this one is immediately struck with its similarity to Ezekiel's portrayal of the twelve gates or exits (48:30-34). Here also there are three gates on every side, each gate representing a different tribe. It is the same in the new Jerusalem for the new Israel of God. Thus we see that there is a continuity between the "church" of the Old Testament and the church of the New Testament.

The twelve angels presiding over the twelve gates in John's vision do not appear in Ezekiel's description. But the idea of watchers, or keepers, at the gates is thoroughly scriptural (cf. II Chron. 8:14 and Isa. 62:6). Their normal function would be to check upon those entering in order to keep out evil persons who might bring destruction from within. Today, we see a carry-over of this idea in fraternal orders, which have officers duly installed to "watch over" the entrance of the place of meeting. Why watchers were needed at the gates of the new Jerusalem to keep out evil is not immediately clear, since all evil has been destroyed. They are, perhaps, symbolic of the righteousness of the city and are vestigial symbols from the past. In our own time gargoyles are sometimes placed on churches even though their original purpose of scaring away demons no longer applies.

The wall of the city not only has twelve gates inscribed with the names of the twelve tribes of Israel; it also has twelve foundations with the twelve names of the twelve apostles of the Lamb written upon them (21:14). Ordinarily one might inquire as to why twelve foundations were needed when one might well have been sufficient; but we do not ask such a question when the statement occurs in an apocalyptic writing. It was the *idea* that the *twelve* foundations suggested that was paramount in the author's mind. Complete apostolic authority undergirded the wall, just as complete Israelitic sanction (the twelve gates) structured it.

The combining of the Hebraic authorities, whether tribes or prophets, with Christian authorities in referring to the basic character of the church appears elsewhere in the New Testament. It was a sound insight that inspired these statements. The God of Moses and the God of Christ were one God in the new creation of the Christian church. Thus the author of Ephesians can speak of the household of God, which is "built upon the foundation of the apostles and prophets" (2:20).

Much is sometimes made of the fact that in speaking of the foundations of the wall as representing the twelve apostles, their individual names are not mentioned. If they had been designated, would Paul's name have been included? Besides this, it is asked, would not Peter have been singled out as the rock (Matt. 16:18)? Who can say? In chapter seven our author named twelve tribes; in referring to the gates of the city, he did not (Ezekiel did so in his reference to the gates cited above). The point seems to me to be a pedantic one, unless John had in mind the corporate character of the church and felt that to name each apostle would have fragmentized it and interfered with his message.

ADORNMENT

In describing the new Jerusalem there are frequent mentionings of certain adornments that add to the brilliance of the scene. It is said that the city as a whole had the glory of God with a "radiance like a most rare jewel, like a jasper, clear as crystal" (21:11). The wall also was built of jasper and the city was pure gold (21: 18). In addition to this "the foundations of the wall of the city were adorned with every jewel" (21:19). Twelve are actually named—jasper, sapphire, agate, emerald, onyx, carnelian, chrysolite, beryl, topaz, chrysoprase, jacinth, and amethyst. We are also told that each of the twelve gates was made of a single pearl, and "the street of the city was pure gold, transparent as glass" (21:21).

What is to be made of these representations? Without any question they were placed here to characterize the beauty and glory of the heavenly city. That they may hold other "hidden" symbolical meanings is also quite likely. They are reminiscent of the breastplate of Aaron (Exod. 28:15 ff.; 39:8 ff.) who as high priest presided over the ceremonies of Israel.[3] Now in heaven they reappear, suggesting their eternal significance. It is not probable that John is here thinking of Christ in terms of his being the great high priest, as in the case of the book of Hebrews. As we shall see, there is no temple in the city; therefore no eternal offering of the sacrifices is necessary or even possible.

There have been occasions in the Apocalypse where it has seemed likely that the author has drawn upon astral forms for his symbolism (12:1 ff.). It is well known that Philo and Josephus have each suggested that the twelve stones on the high priest's breastplate are to be equated with the twelve signs of the zodiac. Rist opines that this may mean that the jewels in the foundations, which are probably based upon Aaron's breastplate, represent stars and that they refer to the saints (Dan. 12:3) who are the martyrs.[4] It is a devious identification, but the mind of an apocalyptist sometimes follows involved patterns of thought.

As a matter of passing interest, it may be pointed out that in the list of beautiful gems we do not always have the counterpart of the jewel that goes by the same name today. For instance, the jasper is not our jasper stone but may refer to an opal or diamond. Such facts do not affect our interpretation of the seer's description of the foundations of the wall. Whatever gem he has in mind, its place in the list is intended to enhance the impression of beauty and magnificence that belongs to the heavenly scene.[5]

[3] Cf. also Ezekiel's description of the splendor of the king of Tyre (28:13) that also seems to have been based upon Aaron's breastplate.

[4] Martin Rist in *The Interpreter's Bible, op. cit.*, p. 537. Cf. also R. H. Charles, *The Revelation of St. John.* (Edinburgh: T. & T. Clark, 1920), II, 165 ff. for the suggestion that John is seeking to Christianize astral references.

[5] For a detailed comparison of the stones here mentioned with their modern counterparts, if there be such, cf. *The Encyclopaedia Biblica* (New York: The Macmillan Company, 1899-1903), IV, 4803 ff. and *A Dictionary of the Bible*, ed. James Hastings (New York: Charles Scribner's Sons, 1902), IV, 619 ff.

THE LIFE WITHIN

Up to this point we have been looking mainly *at the city*, its size, shape, structure, and adornment. What of the life going on within it? This is even more important than its appearance. John has a number of highly significant things to say in this connection. First, there is no temple in the city "for its temple is the Lord God the Almighty and the Lamb" (21:22). Where they are present, no sanctuary is needed; all is temple. In this same sense, with God and the Lamb at the heart of the city, no other illumination is needed; they outshine the brightest of all luminaries, sun and moon alike. The emphasis here is upon *glory* rather than upon physical brightness for "the glory of God is its light, and its lamp is the Lamb" (21:23).[6]

Even the Gentiles enjoy this glory, for they shall enter the gates of the city that are never shut (for the night?); there is no night there (21:24-26). In the face of the events previously described in the Apocalypse, it is difficult to tell where these Gentiles—and also the unclean persons who are mentioned as not being permitted entrance—come from (21:27). On the basis of literary analysis several suggestions have been made to meet this problem, which suggestions involve the adaptation of a Jewish document, redactors, etc. The answer may lie here. On the other hand, this may be just another of the inconsistencies of apocalyptic writings in general and of the book of Revelation in particular. What John has in mind is the purity and universality of the salvation provided for the saints in the new Jerusalem. We are reminded in this reference of the song of the triumph of the Lamb, in which Christ was lauded for ransoming men "from every tribe and tongue and people and nation" (5:9c).

Before ending the description of the glory that belongs within the celestial city, the seer presents a final scene (22:1-5). In it he gathers together the richest symbolism of the Hebrew scriptures—

[6] *The Book of Hymns* (VII, 25) of the Dead Sea Scrolls (*The Dead Sea Scriptures, op. cit.*, p. 162) says of God, "For Thou art unto me as a light eternal keeping my feet upon [the way]." This belongs to the same family of ideas that lies behind this passage in the Apocalypse.

145

words that loving hearts had lingered over in generations past, as he describes the river of the water of life that flows from the throne of God and of the Lamb. They were no doubt familiar to many of his readers since they were based upon the Garden of Eden story in Genesis (2:9 ff.) and upon the vision of Ezekiel who saw waters flow from beneath the temple as a healing stream (47:1-12). Here is the "tree of life" that bears fruit eternally—twelve kinds twelve times a year! Even its leaves are good for healing. Here where there shall be no mourning, no crying, no pain, and no death, there shall also be no want and no sickness. All the things that trouble earth are absent in heaven's own domain.

It is summed up in the closing words of the Revelation proper:

> **There shall no more be anything accursed, but the throne of God and of the Lamb shall be in it, and his servants shall worship him; they shall see his face, and his name shall be on their foreheads. And night shall be no more; they need no light of lamp or sun, for the Lord God will be their light, and they shall reign for ever and ever.**
>
> **—Rev. 22:3-5**

Let us leave it here in all its glory; for there are times when silence is better than speech, when worship and wonder should supplant the words of men. This is the final glory.

CHAPTER TWELVE

Last Words on Last Things

It is important to introduce a subject of great significance in the proper manner; it is important, also, to bring it to a close in a telling fashion. When this is not done, something is taken away from the teaching itself, no matter how weighty and pertinent its contents might be.

This is not simply a question of good taste, decorum, or proper style. There is more here than aesthetics or appropriateness. Certainly in the case of the Apocalypse, with its unfolding drama of judgment and blessing that reveals the final destiny of history, the introduction of the theme and the concluding comments that are made regarding it are not secondary. They belong essentially to the entire prophecy and may not be separated from it without serious loss.

In interpreting the Apocalypse considerable attention is usually given to the introductory chapters, although the prophecy of the future does not properly begin until chapter six. But the concluding verses of the final chapter (22:6-21), usually referred to as the epilogue, are sometimes passed over quickly. Brief summarizations are presented and the discussion is then summarily brought to a close. When this is done, there is a real loss.

INTRODUCTIONS AND CONCLUSIONS

In the book of Revelation the purpose of the introductory chapters is to lead up to the visions of the future. This is intended not only to make an effective approach to the subject matter, but also to carry the reader into the theme. He must be helped to understand what it is all about, to appreciate its great and eternal significance, and to relate it to his own personal situation. John was not writing an abstract treatise; he was addressing himself to the church that was fighting for its life. It was vitally necessary that disillusionment should give way to hope, cynicism to confident expectation. Courage and loyalty to Christ in the midst of actual or threatened persecutions were called for, and the seer was given a message for just such an hour.

The conclusion of the Apocalypse is also related both to ideas and to persons. In a stoccado fashion it touches upon a number of themes that had already been treated at length in the body of the writing, and it reaffirms them and asserts their importance. But more significantly than this, it also addresses the readers with a directness that is unmistakable. It is for them that these words are written, for them as they stand in the midst of a situation involving their eternal destiny.

These last words on last things may be compared to the upper room discourses in the Gospel of John, where Jesus used the final hours of his life to affirm and reaffirm his message to the twelve. There was need to impress upon them the significance of his life, his death on the morrow, and his living presence in the Spirit for days ahead. The brief time at hand for doing this added to the urgency.

It was the same with John. He believed that the end was near (there will be more about this later in the chapter) and that every hour counted for life or death. The prophecy he had presented in his writing had filled him with a sense of crisis. Imagine how it must have felt to have been the vehicle for such announcements as the seer had made. Now, how could he bring all of this home to his readers personally? How could he underline and underscore it one more time before letting it go?

The epilogue is John's attempt to answer this question. It is personal and direct. There is a kind of nervousness about it that reflects the author's eagerness and concern. He seems to turn from one subject to another and back again, as he makes his way to the benediction at the end. These irregularities have led to different theories of the composition of the epilogue.[1] I am considering it in this chapter as coming from John, the author of the Apocalypse itself. These are the final words that he would speak to the church in this farewell note with which the Revelation closes. We can therefore understand their urgent accent.

We might compare the epilogue to the closing paragraphs in the missionary correspondence of Paul. The main body of his argument has been concluded; he must now, as we say, sign off. In this moment the apostle usually becomes quite personal, introducing the names of individuals and giving specific advice to persons who come before his mind's eye. There is sometimes a tenderness that characterizes his tone of writing under these circumstances. Not infrequently there is a note of sharpness or warning. It is the same with John of the Apocalypse.

AUTHENTICATION [2]

Even as at the beginning of the Revelation (1:1, 10 ff.), so now at the end, the seer in the epilogue seeks to authenticate his message. He does not want the charge leveled against it that here are the vain imaginings of a spurious and self-appointed prophet. Therefore, he notes at the very outset of this section that one (presumably Christ or the angel of the preceding paragraph) said to him, "These words are trustworthy and true. And the Lord, the God of the spirits of the prophets, has sent his angel to show his servants what must soon take place" (22:6).

Angels had long been accepted among the Hebrews—particularly since the contacts with Persia—as the intermediaries between heaven and earth. In the Revelation they frequently have brought the divine message to the seer. Even his visions may be regarded as due to the activity of such heavenly angelic agents. In the very opening of the book did not John write, "And he made it known

---

[1] For a helpful analysis and evaluation of these, cf. Beckwith, *op. cit.*, pp. 781-82.

[2] Passages in the epilogue will not be interpreted in this chapter according to the order of their appearance in the Revelation. Instead, they are grouped together in relation to the themes with which they deal. This seemed to me to be preferable in view of the sketchy character of their presentation.

by sending his angel to his servant John" (1:1)? He had just said that God had given him the revelation. Presumably there was no contradiction in his mind beween thinking of God as the source of the prophecy and of an angel as mediating it.

John's message is not only to be regarded as authentic because it came from God's angel; it is also to be considered as final because it came from Jesus himself. This is made quite clear when the seer records the words, "I Jesus have sent my angel to you with this testimony." Then, as though to further identify himself as the Messiah, he adds, "I am the root and the offspring of David, the bright morning star" (22:16). This is the Jesus of history who is speaking. The use of the name itself would indicate this. It was thus that he was known in the days of his flesh.

The word *Jesus* seems to have been a favorite one with John. It is used in fourteen passages in the Apocalypse, and most frequently in referring to Christ as one who bears a witness or reveals a truth. This is what we have in the present case. The fact that he did so through an angel did not mean that he was not the source of the revelation. Even as God had done, Jesus likewise expressed himself through an intermediary heavenly being.

There is a deliberateness that should not be missed in the adding of the identifying statement to the name Jesus, i.e., the reference to the root and offspring of David and to the bright morning star. As we said, Christ is here pointed out as the historic messiah and as such, his ministry in the Revelation is related to the purposes and activity of God in the Old Testament as well as in the New. He is of the house and lineage of David where the hopes and ideals of the messianic age were believed by the Jews to have had their beginning. Paul had helped the church to realize its link to this Hebrew past, where God had begun to express his eternal will through the chosen people. This purpose, in the course of time, had ultimately found its realization in the Christian community. This is evidenced by the fact that it was Jesus, the Jewish messiah, who was now revealing the destiny of men and nations to the church through John the Seer.

The Jesus who was authenticating the revelations was more than the Jewish messiah, however; he was also "the bright morning star." Could it be that these words were intended to offset the hesitancy of some—particularly those in the gentile world—to respond to the Hebraic accents of the reference to David just made? As the bright morning star which was noted for its brilliance in the heavens, shining even in the daylight, Jesus is the light which lightens every man by his coming into the world (John 1:9). He is the universal savior. In this same vein the vision with which the Apocalypse opened—of one like unto a son of man—points to the glory of Christ by saying that "his face was like the sun shining in full strength" (1:16). It shone everywhere.

Behind the reference to the star may lie some characteristic apocalyptic expression. We know that Daniel spoke of the wise who "shall shine like the brightness of the firmament; and those who turn many to righteousness, like the stars for ever and ever" (12:3. Cf. also II Esdras 7:97). And in Second Peter, which contains a marked strain of apocalypticism, the readers are apprised concerning the new day that will dawn when the morning star rises in their hearts (1:19). In any case, the Jesus who authenticates the prophecy calls himself in the epilogue "the bright morning star." As such he speaks with authority to all.[3]

"I AM COMING SOON"

One of the most insistent teachings of the epilogue is that the end of the age is at hand. What John had noted in the very first verse of the Apocalypse when he recorded the words, "What must soon take place" (1:1) is reiterated at least five times in its closing verses (22:6, 7, 10, 12, 20). This is done with deliberate intention. Next to authenticating the prophecy it is the most important word that he utters as he ends his book. Let us look at the several different ways in which it is phrased:

[3] In the Zadokite Document of the Essenes that is now considered as related to the Dead Sea Brotherhood, although it was discovered in Old Cairo in 1896-97 (published 1910), the "star" or "star-god" of Amos 5:26 is said to refer to interpreters of the Law (VII, 14). This provides another illustration of the symbolism that was attached to stars, and suggests an additional area of possible meaning for 22:16. (Cf. *The Dead Sea Scriptures, op. cit.,* p. 70.)

1. ". . . to show his servants *what must soon take place*" (vs. 6).
2. "And behold, *I am coming soon*" (vs. 7).
3. "Do not seal up the words of the prophecy of this book, *for the time is near*" (vs. 10).
4. "Behold, *I am coming soon*" (vs. 12).
5. "He who testifies to these things says, '*Surely I am coming soon*'" (vs. 20).[4]

What could be more definite than this? For all their inherent truth, even the words of the author of Second Peter, when he points out that with the Lord one day is as a thousand years and a thousand years as one day (3:8), cannot dim the impression that the John who wrote the Apocalypse personally expected it to be fulfilled within the immediate future. He sincerely believed that many of those whom he was addressing would witness the coming of Christ, and on this basis he was urging them to be prepared for that great and terrible day of the Lord.

What the seer had in mind in these references to the coming of Christ was the inaugurating of the events that would bring history to a close. The advent from heaven of the faithful and true warrior-Messiah, who would ride a white horse as he led the celestial armies composed of the marytrs against the dragon, his two agents the beasts, and those who followed them, was at hand. *Armageddon was to be current history.* The millennium, the final judgment, and the coming of the new heaven and the new earth with the heavenly city of Jerusalem would follow in due course. The seer's expectation is as definite and specific as this.

In holding this outlook, John was being true to what he regarded as the meaning of the revelations that came to him, which he recorded so painstakingly for the church in his own day and, in the providence of God, for ours. He was also in line with the expectations of primitive and Pauline eschatology which looked toward a return of Christ at the end of the age. This is not the place to discuss the similarities and dissimilarities in the viewpoints of

[4] Italics mine.

Paul and the seer regarding these matters. It is sufficient to note that each anticipated, with Christ's return, a coming crisis that would bring history to a close, reveal the character of God in terms of human destiny, judge the wicked, and bless the faithful forever.[5]

With the writing of the Gospel of John (*ca* A.D. 100-110) this view was later to change somewhat, the emphasis being placed upon the return of Christ in the Spirit that had already occurred. This was evidenced in the new life in Christ that men were already experiencing in the Christian fellowship. But earlier in the century, because of a developing interest in apocalypticism this truth was pushed into the background—although not altogether—in favor of a crisis eschatology. This was particularly true in times of stress and strain, when the Christians were facing persecution. The writing of the book of Revelation during the closing years of the rule of Domitian, with the suffering that accompanied refusal to worship the emperor, is a supreme illustration of this fact.[6] Particularly significant in bearing this out is the almost frantic expectation in the Apocalypse that the end was at hand.

The epilogue, by implication, contains a further word that indicates John's belief in Jesus' imminent return. This is to be found in a statement of the angel, which at first reading may seem almost predestinarian. It is not so intended; instead, it is pointing to the solemn fact that it is too late for sinners to repent and change their lives before Christ comes. The words to which I refer are these: "Let the evildoer still do evil, and the filthy still be filthy" (22:11). They are followed immediately, however, with "and the righteous still do right, and the holy still be holy." Habits are already fixed; change is all but impossible. With the end so near there are no occasions for repentance; neither are there tempta-

---

[5] Cf. the discussion of these matters at the close of chapter two, pp. 35-39. Provocative studies of this theme in relation to the New Testament as a whole may be seen in Paul S. Minear, *Christian Hope and the Second Coming* (Philadelphia: The Westminster Press, 1954) and J. A. T. Robinson, *Jesus and His Coming* (Nashville: Abingdon Press, 1957).

[6] I have dealt with these matters at some length in my unpublished thesis for the doctorate, *The Fourth Gospel—A Reply to the Apocalypse of John*, library of Boston University School of Theology.

tions to apostasy. The reader will recall that it was indicated that this was the presupposition also behind the series of judgments. They were announcements of coming doom rather than evangelistic invitations to turn to Christ.[7]

One word more in this regard. John was instructed not to seal up the words of the prophecy (22:10). This is in direct contrast to Daniel's experience when the one standing before him who had "the appearance of a man" said to him, "The vision of the evenings and the mornings which has been told is true; but seal up the vision" (8:26). The reason for the injunction is also the very opposite. Daniel is advised that the fulfillment of his prophecy is "many days hence"; John, instead, is informed that "the time is near." The first readers who read of *the unsealed prophecy* would be inspired to wait breathlessly for the events that would fulfill it.

WORDS OF BLESSING AND WARNING

In the light of the situation that was facing the church and the attitude of mind that the Revelation itself must have induced, one might conclude that little more needed to be said. Not so. John is not content to let the matter rest until he has added other words of blessing and warning. He presents a beatitude for those who keep the prophecy. They are blessed, indeed (22:7b). It is none other than Christ himself who utters this word, but one has the feeling that it also comes from John the author, who heartily concurs. An almost identical beatitude opened the Apocalypse (1:3), except that here, reading and hearing the divine words that are about to be spoken concerning the future are also enjoined. Statements of this character are typical of apocalyptic writings. Their purpose is to point to the importance of the message that is given.

This is not, however, the only beatitude in the epilogue: there is yet another. It, too, is spoken by Christ who has just referred to himself as the Alpha and the Omega (22:13), a title hitherto reserved only for God himself in the Revelation (1:8; 21:6). Pre-

[7] Cf. p. 87.

viously in the prophecy Christ had been known as "the first and the last" (1:17; 2:8), an expression implying his eternal existence. Now in this reference he is one with God who shall bring "recompense to repay every one for what he has done" (22:12).

In contrast to the severity of Christ's function as judge, this beatitude from his lips (and John's) is beautifully tender. He says, "Blessed are those who wash their robes, that they may have the right to the tree of life and that they may enter the city by the gates" (22:14). This is reminiscent of the proleptic vision in chapter seven (vs. 14) where the seer sees a great company of those who "have washed their robes and made them white in the blood of the Lamb." The tree of life that is in the new Jerusalem is likewise here (22:2), as are also the twelve gates to the celestial city (21:12-14). John may seem to be repeating himself, but he cannot quite let go of the glory he has seen for the faithful. It is too wonderful not to be restated.

As within the body of the prophecy visions of blessing are interlaced with visions of judgment for the purpose of heightening the interest of the readers, so in the epilogue, beatitudes are followed by sober words of caution. John solemnly writes,

> I warn every one who hears the words of the prophecy of this book: if any one adds to them, God will add to him the plagues described in this book, and if any one takes away from the words of the book of this prophecy, God will take away his share in the tree of life and in the holy city, which are described in this book.
>
> —*Rev. 22:18-19*

How like the Old Testament warnings in Deuteronomy: "You shall not add to the word which I command you, nor take from it" (4:2), and "Everything that I command you you shall be careful to do; you shall not add to it or take from it" (12:32).

The similar words in the Apocalypse are intended to keep later readers from perverting the original message. It is not to be toned down or stepped up. There is an eternal sanctity to it the way it stands that must be respected, or the severest of penalties will be imposed. In placing these words at the close of his writing, John is once more expressing his belief in the authority behind them as well as asserting his own faithfulness in reporting the visions.

ASPIRATIONS AND PRAYERS

There is yet another type of expression in the epilogue. We have taken note of authentications, expectations of the approaching fulfillment of the prophecy, and words of blessing and warning. Spiritual aspiration and deep longing of soul are also to be found here. They come from the Spirit (of prophecy) and the Church, or from the Spirit through the Church. Heaven itself wells up from within the body of believers with a glorious prayer: "The Spirit and the Bride say 'Come'" (22:17). It is to Christ as the bridegroom that the Church as the bride makes her petition. The marriage that was announced (19:7 ff.) and foreseen (21:2) had not yet taken place—and could not until the final events that were prophesied were put into motion.

Almost as in liturgical worship, there is a response to this saintly aspiration. Those who hear it uttered join in; they become a praying company of believers who likewise cry "Come." For only when the Bridegroom appears will the thirsty be satisfied with the water of life itself. And like the proffered mercy of God in Isaiah,

"Ho, every one who thirsts,
    come to the waters;
and he who has no money,
    come, buy and eat!
Come, buy wine and milk
    without money and without
        price."

—*Isa. 55:1*

the blessings of the new Jerusalem are free for the faithful.

There is one prayer more before the book of Revelation closes. It is the most significant of all the prayers in the early church:

"Come, Lord Jesus!" (22:20). For this prayer John uses the Greek form of the Aramaic word *Maranatha*. This is probably the oldest of liturgical prayers and it is addressed to Jesus as Lord. We learn from the *Didache* (The Teaching of the Twelve Apostles) that it was said at the end of the meal.[8] It is instructive to note that Paul had already employed it in bringing his letter to the Corinthians to a conclusion, "Our Lord, come!" (I Cor. 16:22). Might not this suggest that this use of the prayer was somewhat customary, since it is also at the close of the Revelation that John places it?

Whatever significance is given to it elsewhere, it is highly appropriate at the end of the Apocalypse. Its appearance here is spontaneous rather than formal. The fulfillment of the entire prophecy as depicted must await the answering of this petition for Christ's return. The Lord has promised it, the Spirit and the Bride have prayed for it; now John the Seer beseeches his Lord that it might be soon—now—at once.

Following the prayer for the Lord's return, the epilogue closes with a brief benediction: "The grace of the Lord Jesus be with all the saints. Amen." (22:21). Until such time as the prophecy comes to pass grace will be needed—grace to persevere, grace to hope, grace to believe the prophecies, grace to overcome. It is the saints who will need this grace, for they are already viewed as being caught up in the trials that immediately precede the end of history.

We have been looking at last words on last things in this chapter. It is with these that the author of the Apocalypse brings his writing to a close; and it is with these, also, that we shall complete our study of the book of Revelation. One is loath to let go of themes so all-encompassing as these we have been considering, particularly since John handles them with such depth of feeling and insight. But the fact is, they will not let go of us so long as we are moved to ask the ultimate questions concerning the purpose of creation and redemption as these are expressed in history, through history, to the end of history—and beyond.

---

[8] Cf. the *Didache* 10:6. This may well be the first formal treatise on church order and should probably be dated around A.D. 100 or shortly after.

I

BIRD'S EYE VIEW OF BIBLE HISTORY [1]
2000 B.C. to A.D. 150 (all dates approximate)

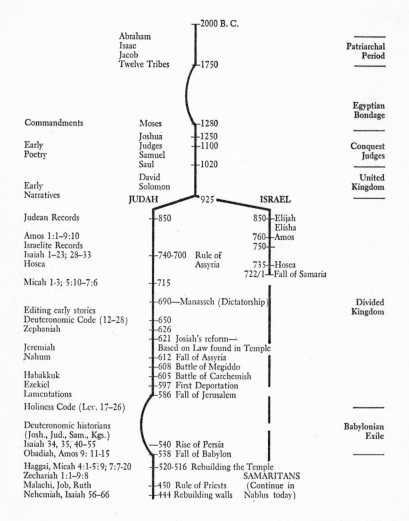

	Abraham	⌐2000 B. C.		
	Isaac			Patriarchal
	Jacob			Period
	Twelve Tribes	⊢1750		
				Egyptian
				Bondage
Commandments	Moses	⊢1280		
	Joshua	⊢1250		
Early	Judges	⊢1100		Conquest
Poetry	Samuel			Judges
	Saul	⊢1020		
	David			United
Early	Solomon			Kingdom
Narratives	**JUDAH**	⊢925	**ISRAEL**	
Judean Records		⊢850	850⊢Elijah	
			Elisha	
Amos 1:1–9:10			760⊢Amos	
Israelite Records			750⊢	
Isaiah 1–23; 28–33		⊢740-700 Rule of		
Hosea		Assyria	735⊢Hosea	
			722/1⊢Fall of Samaria	
Micah 1-3; 5:10–7:6		⊢715		
		⊢690—Manassch (Dictatorship)		Divided
Editing early stories				Kingdom
Deuteronomic Code (12–28)		⊢650		
Zephaniah		⊢626		
		⊢621 Josiah's reform—		
Jeremiah		Based on Law found in Temple		
Nahum		⊢612 Fall of Assyria		
		⊢608 Battle of Megiddo		
Habakkuk		⊢605 Battle of Carchemish		
Ezekiel		⊢597 First Deportation		
Lamentations		⊢586 Fall of Jerusalem		
Holiness Code (Lev. 17–26)				
Deuteronomic historians				Babylonian
(Josh., Jud., Sam., Kgs.)				Exile
Isaiah 34, 35, 40–55		—540 Rise of Persia		
Obadiah, Amos 9: 11-15		⊢538 Fall of Babylon		
Haggai, Micah 4:1-5:9; 7:7-20		⊢520-516 Rebuilding the Temple		
Zechariah 1:1–9:8			SAMARITANS	
Malachi, Job, Ruth		⊢450 Rule of Priests	(Continue in	
Nehemiah, Isaiah 56–66		⊢444 Rebuilding walls	Nablus today)	

---

[1] This outline was prepared by John C. Trever and first appeared in *The International Journal of Religious Education.* It has been revised and is printed here with permission of the author.

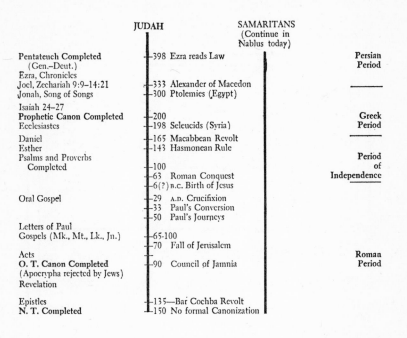

	JUDAH	SAMARITANS (Continue in Nablus today)	
Pentateuch Completed (Gen.–Deut.) Ezra, Chronicles	398 Ezra reads Law		Persian Period
Joel, Zechariah 9:9–14:21 Jonah, Song of Songs	333 Alexander of Macedon 300 Ptolemies (Egypt)		
Isaiah 24–27 Prophetic Canon Completed Ecclesiastes	200 198 Seleucids (Syria)		Greek Period
Daniel Esther Psalms and Proverbs Completed	165 Maccabean Revolt 143 Hasmonean Rule 100		Period of Independence
	63 Roman Conquest 6(?) B.C. Birth of Jesus		
Oral Gospel	29 A.D. Crucifixion 33 Paul's Conversion 50 Paul's Journeys		
Letters of Paul Gospels (Mk., Mt., Lk., Jn.)	65-100 70 Fall of Jerusalem		
Acts O. T. Canon Completed (Apocrypha rejected by Jews) Revelation	90 Council of Jamnia		Roman Period
Epistles N. T. Completed	135—Bar Cochba Revolt 150 No formal Canonization		

II

ROMAN EMPERORS IN THE FIRST CENTURY

Caesar Augustus ...... 27 B.C.–A.D. 14

Tiberius ..............A.D. 14–37

Caligula ............A.D. 37–41

Claudius ............A.D. 41–54

Nero ................A.D. 54–68

Galba ...............A.D. 68–69

Otho ...............A.D. 69

Vitellius ............A.D. 69

Vespasian ...........A.D. 69–79

Titus ...............A.D. 79–81

Domitian ...........A.D. 81–96

Nerva ..............A.D. 96–98

Trajan .............A.D. 98–117

159

III

MAPS

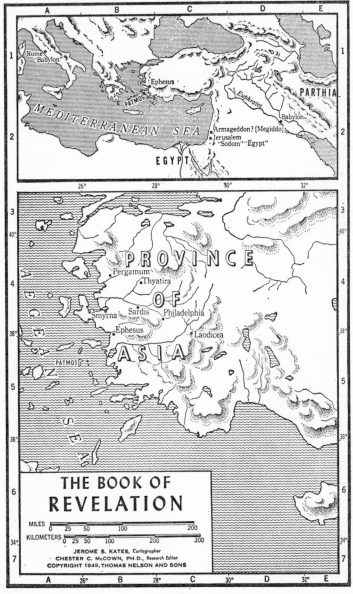

IV

THE SCHEME OF EVENTS IN THE APOCALYPSE [1]

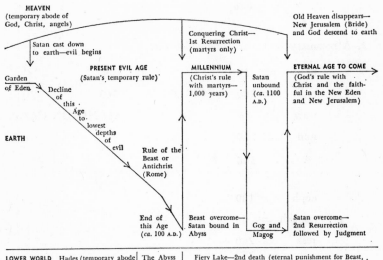

LOWER WORLD	Hades (temporary abode of most of the dead)	The Abyss	Fiery Lake—2nd death (eternal punishment for Beast, Satan, worshiper of Beast, apostate Christians)

V

ATTEMPTS TO SOLVE THE RIDDLE OF 666

Typical reconstructions based on gematria (the assignment of numerical value to letters) of the identification of the beast whose number in the Apocalypse is said to be 666. In some manuscripts the number is given as 616.[2]

1. Two reconstructions based upon Latin:

N =	50	N =	50
E =	6	E =	6
R =	500	R =	500

[1] Taken from Martin Rist as found in *The Interpreter's Bible*, XII, 365, and used with the permission of Abingdon Press.

[2] Cf. the discussion of this question in the text of the book, pp. 58-59.

$$O = 60 \qquad\qquad O = \underline{60}$$
$$N = \underline{50} \qquad\qquad\qquad 616$$
$$666$$

2. A reconstruction based upon Hebrew:

nun	= 50		306
resh	= 200	NERON	360
waw	= 6		666 NERON CAESAR
nun	= 50		
	306		

qoph	= 100	
samekh	= 60	CAESAR
resh	= 200	
	360	

3. A reconstruction based upon the Greek form of the word *Latin* (Lateinos).

$$L = 30$$
$$A = 1$$
$$T = 300$$
$$E = 5$$
$$I = 10$$
$$N = 50$$
$$O = 70$$
$$S = \underline{200}$$
$$666$$

The above was suggested as far back as Irenaeus (*ca.* A.D. 180) and has been frequently used throughout the centuries—including the present. It is interpreted as meaning the Latin church or Roman Catholicism. This reconstruction lacks the historical significance of 1 and 2, because it points beyond a situation contemporary with the writing of the Apocalypse.

4. A misleading reconstruction based upon the words that are said to appear on the front of the pope's crown, in which the numerical value of the letters in terms of Roman numerals is 666. This, it is claimed, identifies the beast with the pope.

V =	5				D =	500
I =	1	F =	0		E =	0
C =	100	I =	1		I =	1
A =	0	L =	50			———
R =	0	I =	1			501
I =	1	I =	1			
V =	5		———			112
S =	0		53			53
	———					501
	112					———
						666

5. An arbitrary reconstruction leading to the name Hitler that was widely circulated during World War II:

A = 100	H = 107
B = 101	I = 108
C = 102	T = 119
D = 103	L = 111
E = 104	E = 104
F = 105	R = 117
G = 106 etc.	———
	666

VI

COSMOGRAPHY IN THE FIRST CENTURY [1]

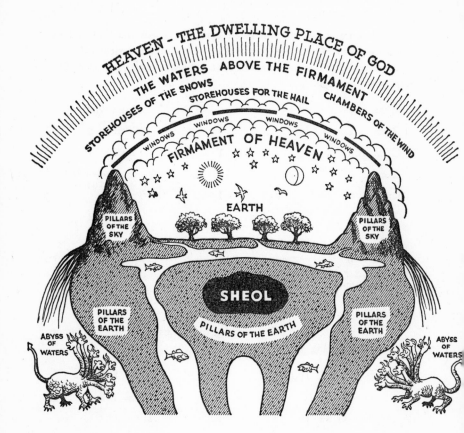

[1] This drawing is taken from the *International Lesson Annual*, 1961, edited by Charles M. Laymon. It is used with the permission of Abingdon Press.

BIBLIOGRAPHY

Allen, Cady H. *The Message of the Book of Revelation*. Nashville: Abingdon-Cokesbury Press, 1939.

Barclay, William. *Letters to the Seven Churches*. Nashville: Abingdon Press, 1957.

Barnett, Albert E. *The New Testament: Its Making and Meaning*. (revised edition). Nashville: Abingdon Press, 1958.

Beckwith, I. T. *The Apocalypse of John*. New York: The Macmillan Company, 1919.

Blair, Edward P. *The Acts and Apocalyptic Literature*. Nashville: Abingdon-Cokesbury Press, 1946.

Bowman, John W. *The Drama of the Book of Revelation*. Philadelphia: The Westminster Press, 1955.

Burnet, A. W. *The Lord Reigneth*. New York: Charles Scribner's Sons, 1947.

Carrington, Philip. *The Meaning of Revelation*. New York: The Macmillan Company, 1931.

Charles, R. H. *The Revelation of St. John*. ("The International Critical Commentary".) 2 vols., Edinburgh: T. & T. Clark, 1920.

Kepler, Thomas S. *The Book of Revelation*. New York: Oxford University Press, 1957.

Kiddle, Martin. *The Revelation of St. John*. ("The Moffatt New Testament Commentary Series.") New York: Harper & Brothers, 1940.

Lilje, Hanns. *The Last Book of the Bible*. Translated by Olive Wyon. Philadelphia: Muhlenberg Press, 1957.

McNeile, A. H. *An Introduction to the Study of the New Testament* (2nd Revised Edition). New York: Oxford University Press, 1953.

Minear, Paul S. *Christian Hope and the Second Coming*. Philadelphia: The Westminster Press, 1954.

Phillips, J. B. (tr.) The Book of Revelation, *The New Testament in Modern English*. New York: The Macmillan Company, 1957.

Rist, Martin and Hough, Lynn Harold. *The Interpreter's Bible*, Nashville: Abingdon Press, 1957. XII.

Robinson, J. A. T. *Jesus and His Coming*. Nashville: Abingdon Press, 1957.

Rowley, H. H. *The Revelance of Apocalyptic*. London: Lutterworth Press, 1944.

Scott. C. A. A. *Revelation*. The Century Bible. New York: Henry Froude, 1925.

Scott, E. F. *The Book of Revelation*. New York: Charles Scribner's Sons, 1940.

Swete, H. B. *The Apocalypse of St. John*. London: Macmillan and Company, Ltd., 1922.

Torrey, Charles C. *The Apocalypse of John*. New Haven: Yale University Press, 1958.

Wernecke, H. H. *The Book of Revelation Speaks to Us*. Philadelphia: The Westminster Press, 1954.

Wishart, Charles Frederick. *The Book of Day*. New York: Oxford University Press, 1935.

INDEX OF REFERENCES

Old Testament

New Testament

Early Noncanonical Writings

INDEX OF SUBJECTS